THE FRICK COLLECTION

Anshen Transdisciplinary
Lectureships in Art, Science and
the Philosophy of Culture

MONOGRAPH FOUR

Previously Published:

Monograph One
THE REAL DISCOVERY OF AMERICA:
MEXICO, NOVEMBER 8, 1519
by
Hugh Thomas

Monograph Two
THE ORIGIN OF THE UNIVERSE
AND THE ORIGIN OF RELIGION
by
Sir Fred Hoyle

Monograph Three
LANGUAGE AND THOUGHT
by
Noam Chomsky

# MAN AND IMAGES IN THE ANCIENT NEAR EAST

## by *Edith Porada*

MOYER BELL

WAKEFIELD, RHODE ISLAND & LONDON

Published by Moyer Bell

Copyright © 1995 by Edith Porada

First Edition

LIBRARY OF CONGRESS
CATALOGING-IN-PUBLICATION DATA

Porada, Edith, 1912–1994
    Man and images in the ancient
    Near East / by Edith Porada. —
    1st ed.
        p.      cm. — (Anshen trans-
    disciplinary lectureships in art,
    science, and the philosophy of
    culture ; monograph 4)
        1. Art, Ancient—Iraq.
    2. Art—Iraq.   3. Art and
    society—Iraq.   I. Title.
    II. Series.
    N5370.P77   1995
    709'.35—dc20          94–43297
                                    CIP
    ISBN 1-55921-129-6 (cl) 1995
    ISBN 1-55921-130-X (pb) 1996

Printed in the United States of America
Distributed in North America by Publishers
Group West, P.O. Box 8843, Emeryville CA
94662 800-788-3123 (in California 510-658-
3453) and in Europe by Gazelle Book
Services Ltd., Falcon House, Queen Square,
Lancaster LA1 1RN England 524-68765.

EDITH PORADA

# IN CELEBRATION OF A LIFE

# CONTENTS

# INTRODUCTION

On behalf of the Trustees and staff of The Frick Collection, I am honored once again to welcome you to an Anshen Transdisciplinary Lectureships in Art, Science, and the Philosophy of Culture. This lecture, the fourth, is, however, tinged with sadness, since our speaker this evening, Dr. Edith Porada, is unable to be with us. She is critically ill; she is, however, wonderfully cared for in Hawaii by her sister, and on behalf of those who are gathered here, I send our love, all of our best wishes, and our very warmest regard.

Dr. Porada's lecture will be presented this evening by Professor John Russell of Columbia University, who is especially renowned for his book on Sennacherib's palace at Nineveh, which last year won the Wiseman Book Award of the Archaeological Institute of America. Professor Russell has been a close associate of Dr. Porada in research, discussion and publication. He represents a continuity of Edith Porada's career at Columbia and everything that she has accomplished there in the field of ancient Near Eastern art and archaeology. We are deeply grateful to Professor Russell and to two other colleagues of Dr. Porada, Sidney Babcock and Prudence Harper, for all of their help during the time of her illness. We also are thankful to Professor Franciscus Wiggermann for coming from The Netherlands to contribute to the discussion of the paper prepared by Dr. Porada.

Professor Wiggermann, a native of Amsterdam, has taught Assyriology at the Free University of Amsterdam since 1974. His interdisciplinary approach combines the skills of a specialist in ancient Near Eastern languages with a knowledge of and curiosity about archaeological artifacts and images. His publications, above all those on Mesopotamian protective spirits, have expanded our knowledge and understanding of the ancient Near Eastern world and our ability to interpret, with some confidence, the works of art.

Professor Wiggermann's research and writings immediately brought him to the attention of Edith Porada, and their collaboration during the past decade has been a most productive one—leading her to ask him on the occasion of her Anshen lecture to provide a commentary and response.

Dr. Ruth Anshen, founder of the Anshen Transdisciplinary Lectureships, a noted philosopher, has been keenly involved in every aspect of these lectureships. Since we gathered here for the third lecture, just ten months ago, she had edited Professor Noam Chomsky's paper presented then, and this has already been published under her guidance. Her attention to details of the work for this program is indefatigable; her passion for investigating the unitary structure of nature and all reality is unending. She has been, I believe, very particularly involved in the lecture which you are about to hear. Her friendship for Edith Porada and her empathy for every aspect of the creation and development of this lecture have resulted in an extraordinary and poignant bond between these two scholars.

Dr. Porada has written: "For as long as I can remember, whether it was in the townhouse in Vienna or in my father's hunting lodge in the summers, I have liked things that could tell one something about their past, like petrified shells or stones." (I quote from her memoir as a scholar of ancient Near Eastern art and archaeology which is appended to the lecture published here.) I know that I speak for hundreds, even thousands of Dr. Porada's students, co-workers, and colleagues, who have benefited from her amazing interest in objects of the very distant past. We have all profited from her synthesizing power in creating vast worlds—artistic, cultural, political, economic—from the tiniest relics of that past. The lecture tonight has been Dr. Porada's all-absorbing interest for the past year. We are fortunate, indeed, in being able to hear it from John Russell, and to have her great friend and colleague Ruth Nanda Anshen introduce it.

—Charles Ryskamp

# PREFACE

In some remote region of our consciousness unity whispers that everything exists at the courtesy of everything else. In other words there can be no separation of subject from object. The unity of nature must be postulated, for if it did not exist, if there were no inherent unity and consistency in nature, there would be no possibility of knowledge.

We are concerned with the unitary structure of all nature. At the beginning, as we see in Hesiod's Theogony and in the Book of Genesis, there was a primal unity, a state of fusion in which, later, all elements become separated but then merge again. However, out of the unity there emerges the separation of parts of opposite elements. These opposites intersect, reunite in meteoric phenomena and in individual living things. Yet, in spite of the immense diversity of creation a profound underlying convergence exists in all nature. And the principle of the conservation of energy simply signifies that there is a *something* that remains constant, and we say that the law of conservation is the physical expression of the elements by which nature makes itself known to us.

It is not enough to consider the mutual entanglement of nature and humanity in relation to aesthetic feeling or the perception of beauty. We are summoned to re-examine all aspects of human endeavor which the specialist was taught to believe he could safely leave aside. It is then that we discover the structural kinship between subject and object; the indwelling of the one in the other. We see that present and past achievements impinge on human life and envisage what we may yet attain when summoned by an unbending inner necessity to the quest of what is most exalted in us.

The existence of knowledge and its astounding consistency (in spite of occasional, partial, temporary contradictions) prove the unity of knowledge and the unity of nature. Even though the building up of knowledge has been done and continues today by people of various races, and many cultures, inspired by different faiths, speaking different languages, proves that these thinkers have the same needs and aspirations, that they reason in the same way, and, as far as they collaborate with each other, they are united. In as much as all knowledge aims at the same general purpose, all efforts of the mind do converge and harmonize.

The unity of humanity as a species is an underlying reality which no individual differences can obliterate. The unity of nature, the unity of knowledge, and the unity of humanity are but three aspects of a single reality. Each aspect helps to justify the others. That trinity is but the dispersion of a fundamental unity which is beyond our material grasp but within our human hearts and minds.

Human knowledge is of course very imperfect, not only in the past but even now and later, it will always be imperfect but it is paradoxically indefinitely perfectible. The imperfection of knowledge is explained and to some extent mitigated by its humanity.

Scientific results are always abstractions and they tend to become more and more abstract, hence they lose their humanity. A scientific theory may be as beautiful as the Hagia Sophia, once a mosque but now a museum, in Turkey. Science can be as human as art or religion, its humanity is implicit, it takes a scientifically educated humanist to draw it out, just as it takes an educated historian of art to draw out the humanity of great art. The same is true of music.

Religions exist because human beings are hungry for goodness, for justice, for compassion or mercy; the arts exist because human beings are hungry for beauty. Knowledge exists because human beings are hungry for truth.

Think of a triangular pyramid; the people standing on different places near the base may be very *distant* from one another but they come nearer as they climb higher. The pyramid symbolizes a new kind of trinity culminating at the pinnacle in unity since it demonstrates that the history of knowledge includes the most glorious, the purest, and most noble achievements of the creative spirit and energy of the mind. The history of humanity's approach to truth is also the history of our approach to peace. There can be no peace anywhere without justice or without truth. These attributes are the joy and pride of the human spirit.

The creative mind looks at things, at the universe of

visible Being intent to grasp in it some reality beyond appearance and some hidden meaning. Natural appearances are totally transformed by the mind into images which pertain to another world since the mind is like the aspirations of an alchemist transmuting lead into gold. But where the alchemist fails, Professor Porada succeeds through her infallible intuition and transcendent creativity in reconciling the particle with the whole, the unitary structure of all reality, into a harmonic unity as in a Bach Fugue, a cosmic principle and a transformation of her objects into meaning, the inanimate into the animate and the invisible into the visible.

And finally we are aware of the spiritual unconscious as we find in concepts, ideas and images analogous to the freedom of the child, the freedom of play, and the freedom of dreams, in other words, the freedom of the creative spirit.

As Edith Porada herself has written in her lecture in this monograph, "an intensity of ancient Near Eastern art prevails and will continue to communicate this intensity to future generations."

I feel that it is appropriate for me to conclude for all of us our gratitude to Sidney Babcock. His devotion to Dr. Porada expresses itself by his extraordinary, indefatigable achievement in collaborating with me in the preparation of this monograph: *Man and Images in the Ancient Near East*, her bequest to art, knowledge, history and culture. Only the perceptive sensibility and Mr. Babcock's unique scholarship, his inimitable dedication to Truth, Beauty and Goodness could bless us with this last great work of our beloved Edith Porada and proves that there is no death—there is only transition.

—Ruth Nanda Anshen

# MAN AND IMAGES
# IN THE ANCIENT
# NEAR EAST

# MAN AND IMAGES IN THE ANCIENT NEAR EAST

First, I want to express my profound thanks to Dr.
Ruth Anshen and Dr. Charles Ryskamp for having invited
me to give one of the lectures in the Anshen Transdisciplinary Series of Lectures in Art, Science and the Philosophy of Culture. Ever since the invitation was tended, two
years ago, it has meant for me an opportunity to present
my field and my ideas about it to a group of persons of
many achievements and interests other than the art of the
ancient Near East. The group, like many educated people in
many fields, had to be convinced that the art of the
ancient Near East is not a curious sideline of world art but
an inherent part with a reality of its own. I have found the
work of the commentator, Frans Wiggermann, most stimu-
lating for my own work and have therefore asked Dr.
Anshen and Dr. Ryskamp to invite him to provide extensions of or contradictions to my text.

The images that will be discussed here are taken from

Greater Mesopotamia which included Iran in the late fourth millennium B.C. The earliest texts of Mesopotamia are in Sumerian followed by the Semitic Akkadian in the second half of the third millennium B.C.

I preface my essay on images and man by presenting the Sumerian concept of the creation of humanity. The text of the following quotations is taken from an article by Wilfred Lambert.[1] "The myth begins with the separation of heaven and earth, and follows with the births and further procreation of the gods, which results in a shortage of food. The senior gods put the junior to work digging canals to make farming productive, a hard labor about which they complained. . . . Enki (god of the sub-terranean freshwater, [Figs. 1, 2] associated with wisdom and magic)[2] and his mother Namma proceed to deal with the situation."

The image of the god Enki, the Ea of the Akkadians, created about 2200 B.C. by Akkadian seal cutters shows the god in his palace formed by the subterranean waters in Fig. 1,[3] and flanked by nude heroes with six curls, his adjuncts, in Fig. 2.[4]

The translation of the Sumerian text reads:

> Namma, the primeval mother who gave birth to the great gods,
> Brought (news of) the weeping of the gods to her son,
> Lord you are reclining, you are sleeping indeed.
> . . . rise.
> The gods you created are smashing (?)
> My son, arise from your bed, with your expertise you must seek out skill.

Fig 1. The water-god in his subterranean palace. Modern impression of a cylinder seal from Ur, Akkadian, ca. 2200 B.C., now in the British Musuem. Photograph by Edith Porada. Originally published in C. L. Woolley, *Ur Excavations* II: The Royal Cemetery (London: The British Museum, 1934), pl. 215, no. 364.

Fig 2. The water-god with attendants. Modern impression of a cylinder seal, Akkadian, ca. 2200 B.C.. The Pierpont Morgan Library, No. 202.

Create a substitute for the gods so that they will be
relieved of their toil.
Enki rose from his bed at the command of his mother
Namma.
In Halanku, his conference chamber he [slapped] his
thigh.
Being expert in wisdom, discernment and consulta-
tion, he produced skill of blood, bodies and cre-
ativity, the birth goddesses.
Enki stationed them at his side, seeking out wisdom.
After Enki had in wisdom reflected upon his own
blood and body
He addressed his mother Namma.
My mother there is my/the blood which you set
aside, impose on it the corvée of the gods.
When you have mixed it in the clay from above the
Apsu[5]
The birth goddesses will nip off the clay and you
must fashion bodies.
Your companion Ninmah will act and will assist as
you bring to birth.
My mother, you decree their destiny so that Ninmah
may impose their corvee.

The image of King Ur-Nammu of Ur, 2112–2095 B.C., in
a foundation figurine, [Figs. 3a and b][6] carrying the basket
of earth and bricks for the temple, the lowliest occupation
on the social scale in Mesopotamia, illustrates the corvée
imposed on mankind.

The concept of original man modeled from clay to
which was mixed a divine substance that brought him to
life is basic to the idea shared by Sumerians and later

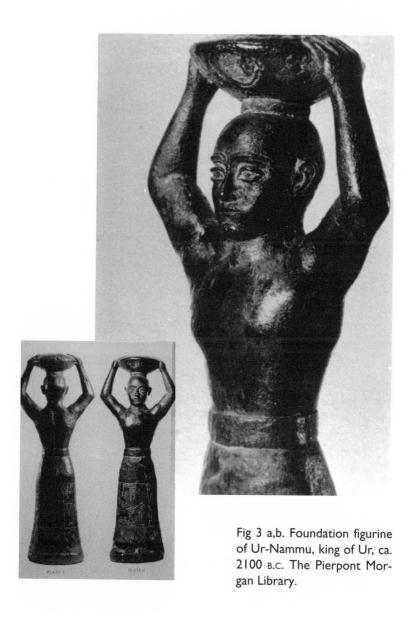

Fig 3 a,b. Foundation figurine of Ur-Nammu, king of Ur, ca. 2100 B.C. The Pierpont Morgan Library.

Fig. 4. Lions of Mari, tentative reconstruction (after D. Beyer, p. 84, fig. 7, see my text, note 7).

Babylonians and Assyrians in Mesopotamia. They believed that active beings could be created from clay if the proper magic formulas were applied. Of course, large works were made of stone or copper over a wooden core like the lions of Mari, tentatively restored by Dominique Beyer inside the cella of the "King of the country." [Fig. 4][7]

Not only modeled and sculptured forms were taken to have inherent power but also figures carved and drawn. Late Babylonian texts show that monsters in protective function drawn, probably, on gates of a house could ward of evil demons.[8] They were surely less well carved but similar in intent to the lion-demons with crossed weapons guarding the entrance in one of the rooms of the North Palace of Ashurbanipal at Nineveh (668–627 B.C.) [Fig. 5].

We will begin our survey of man and images in the

Fig. 5. Lion-demons crossing weapons, relief from the North Palace of Ashurbanipal (after a drawing by Cl. Wolff in *Reallexikon der Assyriologie und vorderasiatischen Archäologie* Bd.7, p. 101, Abb. 1).

ancient Near East, however, at the stage before the making of images. This takes us back to the Middle Paleolithic period about 40,000 B.C. when people lived in small groups, probably within a world of thought related to that of modern Shamanism. The name is derived from the spiritual life of some of the Ural-Altaic peoples. Their Shamanism was actually terminated by the Soviets, but earlier, in the 18th and 19th centuries, their customs were occasionally observed with interest and recorded, as by the Dutch trader, Nikolas C. Witsen. [Fig. 6].

Fig. 6. Drawing of a performance by a stag-horned Shaman (after Nikolas C. Witsen, *Noord en Oost Tartaryen*, Amsterdam, 1692).

I now cite from an article by Prokofyeva which describes the meaning of the details in the costumes of an Enets (eastern Samoyed) Shaman.[9] She says: "up to our times the Enets have preserved in their religious beliefs ancient animistic concepts. . . . The entire world (*i.e.* the sky and the earth) was populated by various spirits, who were responsible for good luck in hunting, health, and the life of man. The Shamans served as "mediators"

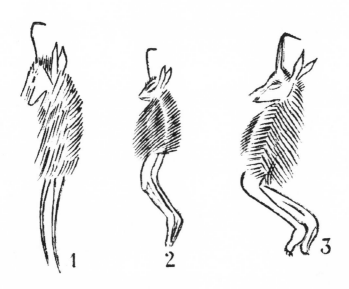

Fig. 7. Chamois-masked dancers (after P. Graziosi, *Die Kunst der Altstein-zeit*, Stuttgart: W. Kohlhammer, 1956, pl.87:f).

between the people and the spirits."[10] I use this brief and simplified description to which we may add the one given by Esther Pasztory, who wrote in her article, "Shamanism and North American Art,"[11] "the religious specialist, called shaman, mediated between humans and the supernatural by going into a trance. During this trance he may take the form of an animal helping-spirit and journey to the upper world or the lower world in order to cure sickness by recapturing lost souls, to conduct the dead to their final resting place, or to communicate with the supernaturals who control nature."[12] Some general features obviously united the Shamanism of different continents, such as the fact that the Shaman's function was that of a healer and that he could fly.

Shamanism was not an organized religion with a fixed place of worship and an established priesthood, hence there was no fixed tradition of image making.[13] If there were ceremonies for the well-being of the small communities of hunters and gatherers, which can be assumed for that state, it was probably in the form of a masked dance, perhaps rendered by upper paleolithic drawings of chamois-masked dancers [Fig. 7].[14]

Fig. 8. Photograph of the discovery of bones of bird wings and goat heads at Shanidar. Courtesy Rose L. Solecki.

I believe that we may have the traces of a stage related to Shamanism in a deposit discovered by Rose and Ralph Solecki at the site of Shanidar in Iraq, a Neanderthal period site of about 40,000 B.C. In that deposit there were the skeletons of the wings

Fig. 9. Goat-man, ca. 3000 B.C., on loan from Robin B. Martin to the Brooklyn Museum.

of gigantic birds of prey together with the heads of goats [Fig. 8].[15] Rose Solecki was convinced that the deposit was of a ceremonial or ritual character and related it to a painting from Chatal Hüyük in Anatolia, dated ca. 6500–5700 B.C.[16] Another association, however, can be made with a copper figure of a man wearing a cap topped by goat's horns and ears and, on his back, the slough of a big bird [Fig. 9a,b].[17]

In an article published in 1992,[18] I suggested that we

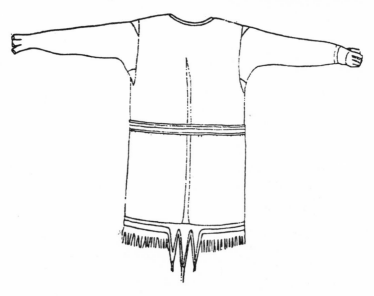

Fig. 10. Back of an Enets Shaman's coat: the center portion of the back hem with three wedge-shaped projections, called "the bird's tail" (after Prokofyeva, p. 128, Figure 2, see my text, note 9).

might have here some retention of shamanistic tradition but I had not reread the detailed description of "The Enets Shaman's Coat". The most important feature is the

drawing of the center portion of the back hem which forms three wedge-shaped projections and is called "the bird's tail" [Fig. 10]. A comparison of the back view of the copper figure [Fig. 11] with the drawing [Fig. 10] shows that it is indeed a bird's skin which hangs on the goat man's back. Another confirmation that a bird's skin was meant in the coat is that fringing, similar to that of the hem, occurs also on the elbow side of the sleeve [Fig. 12] with the same meaning of "feathers". Thus the coat of the Enets and several related groups symbolizes a bird, or rather the skin of a bird, we may repeat, like the object on the back of our copper figure.

This heavy figure seems to stand weightlessly on

Fig. 11. Goat-man, back view with bird's tail.

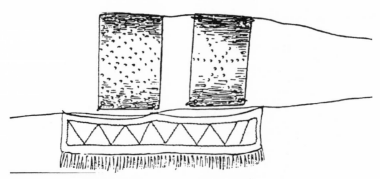

Fig. 12. Fringing of the sleeves of the Enets Shaman's coat, representing feathers (after Prokofyeva, p. 129, Figure 3).

Fig. 13. Goat-man, side view showing the boots upturned in front.

shoes with upturned tips [Fig. 13] that are characteristic of those worn by ancient Near Eastern mountain peoples as in a cylinder seal of about 3000 B.C. from Nineveh in the British Museum [Fig. 14] though the shoes are greatly exaggerated in the figure, suggesting the figure's magically speedy advance.

The intensity of the figure's facial expression and the taughtness of the position of this fully modeled figure are achievements of the later period [Fig. 15], about 3400–3000 B.C., called Uruk after the Early Bronze Age town of that name. While the Martin figure in the Brooklyn Museum and another in the Albright Gallery of Buffalo thus belong to the Uruk style, their appearance may reflect features of early Shamans of prehistory, as shown above, although their meaning may have changed under the influence of the man-centered atmosphere of the Uruk period.

Fig. 14. Drawing of an impression of a cylinder seal from Kujundjik (Nineveh), late Uruk style, ca. 3000 B.C., showing a huntsman with boots upturned in front (after Pierre Amiet, *La glyptique mésopotamienne archaïque*. 2nd ed. Paris, 1980, No. 1588, plate 119).

We return once more to the Siberian Shamans and a group related to the Enets, the Selkup, whose "shamanistic songs describe how and where the spirits fly in the following manner: At the invitation of the Shaman . . . the principal spirit bird, the eagle (or crane) arrives; behind it fly the lesser spirit birds . . . a number hide themselves under the wings of the large [principal] bird." This image of a large bird with small spirit birds in its wings and feathers is imitated in the costume of the Enets

Fig. 15. Goat-man, detail, showing intensity of expression.

Shaman, where the braids evidently also are feathers.[19] The carving of a spear thrower of reindeer antler of an adult bird with nestling from the late Magdalenian site of Enlène in France (ca. 14,000–11,000 B.C.) [Fig. 16][20], suggests a relationship of concepts about the role and power of great birds over continents and millennia.

We return to Mesopotamia with the earliest carvings so far published from that country dated about 10,000–8,000 B.C., excavated by Stefan K. Kozlowski. They are small heads of birds on long necks found at the site of Nemriq, a settlement with architectural remains.[21] One of the birdheads, made of cream colored hard limestone or marble [Fig. 17], is beautifully sculptured. The other bird heads [like Fig. 18] are made of pebbles and, according to Kozlowski, are unfinished. Were they connected in some way with concepts about birds in a Shamanistic tradition? We don't know, but we can keep all these facts in mind and a next generation may ask why we did not see the obvious.

A snake and a leopard are said by Kozlowski to have been among additional finds at Nemriq.[22] Thus the most powerful animals—eagle, leopard, and snakes—were represented. Here we may already have a transition from originally Shamanistic ideas to their transposition into permanent form as some of the people had formed a sedentary population.

The works of about 8000 to 6000 B.C. are rare; we get a

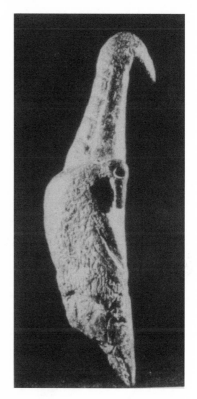

Fig. 16. Spear thrower hook, carved from reindeer antler: large bird with small bird under its wing, late Magdalenian, ca. 14,000–11,000 B.C. (after Randall White, "The Earliest Images: Ice Age 'Art' in Europe," *Expedition* 34/no. 3, 1992, p. 47, fig.14).

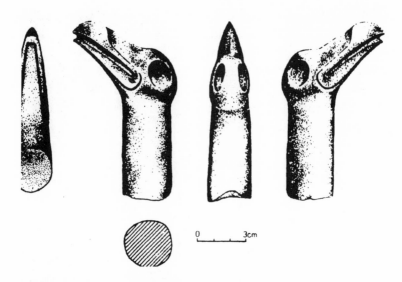

Fig. 17. Bird head of hard limestone or marble from Nemriq, Iraq, ca. 10,000–8,000 B.C. (after Stefan K. Kozlowski, *Nemriq 9*, p. 155, Fig. 64).

Fig. 18. Unfinished bird head of pebble or sandstone from Nemriq, Iraq (after Kozlowski, *Nemriq 9*, p. 156, Fig. 65).

– 156 –

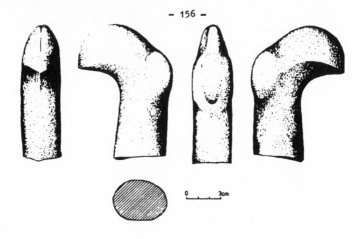

Fig. 19. Beaker with two snakes from Susa I, ca. 4000 B.C. (after *The Royal City of Susa: Ancient Near Eastern Treasures in the Louvre held at the Metropolitan Museum of Art, Nov. 1992-March 1993*, p. 35, cat. no. 3).

better idea of the purpose for which objects of art were made from the pottery and stamp seals that were produced in large numbers from the sixth millennium B.C. onward.

For us, the most meaningful representations on pottery and seals derive from the latter part of the Ubaid period, ca. 4500–3500 B.C. The pots come from Susa in Iran. On the great beaker [Fig. 19], we see only two serpents. There is only one fragment of the head of a similar serpent known to me from Susa.[23] There are no other representations from Susa in which a serpent is recognizable by the head of the reptile.[24]

Serpents also occur on stamp seals, the practical use of which is well known: their impressions secured containers and entrances through doors to store rooms. Large

Fig. 20. Seal impression from Susa A: showing a goat-headed figure with serpents (after Amiet, *Glyptique mésopotamienne archaique*, pl. 6, No. 118).

Fig. 21. Seal impression from Susa, level 25: goat-headed figure with serpents (after Amiet, *Glyptique mésopotamienne archaique*, pl. 115, No. 1530).

stamp seals, however, with special representations may have been worn as emblems of distinction as seen perhaps on the impression of a stamp seal with a goat-headed figure from Susa [Fig. 20]. This and another impression of a stamp seal, found in a recent, carefully stratified excavation, in level 25, dated about 3500 B.C., [Fig. 21] show the subject of a goat-man or demon with serpents. The motif was also represented on one example at Tepe Gawra in northern Mesopotamia[25] and in another at Tell Asmar in the center of the country.[26] Many such stamps have no precise provenience except a general origin in Western Iran.[27] With the widely distributed motif involving serpents it almost seems as if the stress on birds had given way to one on serpents.[28] In the numerous representations of a demon with the head of a goat or a moufflon, he either grasps the serpents or stands between them with hands raised as in a posture, perhaps of conjuration [as in Fig. 22]. There are also birds, boars, and dogs, even fish, represented with a goat-headed figure, but snakes constitute the majority of the designs. Whichever superhuman personage may be represented by the horned figure between the serpents, it was certainly a being that could influence them, hence, it must have been thought to ward off serpents and their bite, which was one of the greatest dangers facing early man in Iran and Mesopotamia in the time of the village cultures of the Ubaid period when agriculture was developed and people worked in the fields, probably barefoot. In seals of the following Uruk period, ca. 3500–3000 B.C., some stamp seals convey this graphically by showing the soles of nude feet, occasionally as at Tell Brak in North Syria, [Fig. 23] highly stylized, and separated by a winding serpent. We can therefore regard such stamp seals with images of serpents as protective amulets against the bite of these reptiles.

Fig. 22. Stamp seal: moufflon-headed demon (after P.R.S. Moorey, E. Porada, E. C. Bunker, and G. Markoe, *Los Angeles County Museum: Ancient Bronzes, Ceramics and Seals,* Los Angeles County Museum of Art, 1981, No. 1010, p. 199).

Fig. 23. Stamp seal: soles of feet and a serpent from Tell Brak (after M.E.L. Mallowan, "Excavations at Brak and Chagar Bazar." *Iraq* 9, 1947, pl. 18, 1).

Are the slit-eyed, earless slender beings in the graves of the Ubaid period of Mesopotamia [Fig. 24] derived from serpent forms? Are the oval patches on the shoulders of the figurines meant to indicate scales? These are probably unanswerable questions. From what has been said about the purpose of the image of a horned demon with snakes on stamp seals it is obvious that the driving emotion in the making of such images was fear of bodily harm and an effort to find protection through the representation of the relevant superhuman figure.

Into the cycle of figures with features of serpents belongs this snake-man [Fig. 25 a, b], again one of two such figures, the other in

Fig. 24. Female figure with reptile(?) head , ca. early fourth millennium B.C. (after Eva Strommenger, *5000 Years of the Art of Mesopotamia*, New York, 1964, Fig. 10)

the Iraq Museum from a known site in Iraq.[29] The present one is in the Cincinnati Art Museum. Like the goat-man the figure can be stylistically dated in the late Uruk

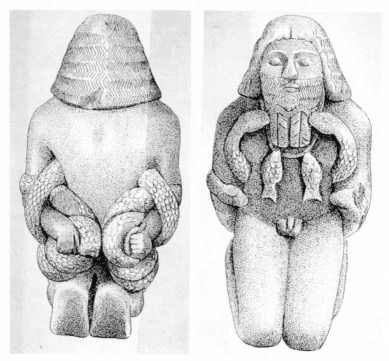

Fig. 25. Snake-man, Late Uruk period, Cincinnati Art Museum (after Porada, Fig. 8 and 9, pl. 76, see my text, note 29).

period, before 3000 B.C. I published the figure in 1992 and described it as bound by serpents. I was influenced by the posture of the foreign captive of the VIth Egyptian Dynasty in the Metropolitan Museum of Art.[30] In the forgery of the snake-man,[31] the modern sculptor obviously

Fig. 26, 27: Chlorite vase with scenes in relief, ca. 2700 B.C., British Museum (after Strommenger, *5000 Years,* Fig. 38).

Fig. 28. Nude heroes with curls, adjuncts of the water god. Modern impression of a cylinder seal, Akkadian, ca. 2200 B.C., formerly in the Moore Collection. Photograph by David Loggie.

thought that the figure was bound by the serpents.[32] In the course of the preparation of this essay on images, and in conversation with colleagues and members of my seminar,[33] I came to realize that the relationship between the serpents and this man is not inimical, he is not bound, he holds the serpents close to his body, his legs restrain the tails of two of the serpents.[34] At first, I thought that he is the master of the serpents, but in the above-mentioned seminar, Laurie Sackler suggested, instead, a relationship between two major powers. The four serpents of the sculpture [Fig. 25 a, b] may represent not only the dangerous reptiles but, at the same time, the life-giving water as in the chlorite vessel in the British Museum of a

Fig. 29. Scenes in a leather (?) workshop in a temple. Modern impression of a cylinder seal, Uruk, ca. 3300 B.C. The Pierpont Morgan Library, No. 1.

later period, perhaps about 2700 B.C. [Fig. 26, 27]. There a figure holds on one side serpents over lions and, on the other side, the same figure holds water courses over bulls. The similarity of their undulating forms indicates their identity. I now think that the snake-man represents an early version of the iconographical figure of the nude bearded hero with six curls. Wiggermann calls this type of figure *laḫmu*.[35] In an art historical context like the present one, however, I insist on the immediately intelligible descriptive name used in English and German: "the nude bearded hero with curls." In later Babylonian religious texts the *laḫmu* were a group of 50 servants of the god Enki (Akkadian Ea). An Akkadian cylinder of about 2200 B.C. [Fig. 28], formerly in the Moore collection, illustrates the main spheres of these nude bearded heroes with curls. The fish, hanging from our figure's necklace fit nicely into that iconography.

In the course of the third millennium B.C. serpents diminish in the iconography of Mesopotamia. This may be taken to render the ideas and the imagery of the people in towns less prone to suffer the attacks of serpents.

Fig. 30. Boat carrying a ruler before a bull with an altar. Modern impression of a cylinder seal from Uruk (after Strommenger *5000 Years*, Fig. 17, third from the top).

However, in the Uruk period, before 3000 B.C., to which we now return, serpents still appear on some cylinder seals, the seal shape introduced at that time together with writing. In the often reproduced cylinder of the Morgan Library, No. 1 [Fig. 29], serpents have been combined with felines to become serpo-felines, a type also known in Egyptian art as on the ceremonial palette of Narmer.[36] On the Uruk period seal the serpo-felines appear to be architectural decoration. The scene has been interpreted as picturing activities in a leather workshop, because of the boot on the ground. Other interpretations, however, are possible.

As pointed out by Wiggermann, in his recent book,[37] monsters are a product of regular artistic activity. In turn, works of art were the result of organized religion. Although the beginnings of organized religions and art lie in the preceding periods, the age of the Uruk period marks the beginning of a continuous iconography in the artistic development of ancient Mesopotamia and Iran. The most

Fig. 31. Stele from Uruk: a ruler killing lions, ca. 3000 B.C. (after Strommenger, *5000 Years*, Fig. 18).

49

impressive scenes on cylinders of the Uruk period evolve not around animals, or animal-headed demons, as do the stamp seals, but around a ruler in various actions: religious, ritual, [Fig. 30], militaristic or in scenes of the hunt. On a stele of the period [Fig. 31] he is shown killing lions. Here the lion appears for the first time as the enemy of man in a truly adversarial relationship. The representation of the ruler on the stele and also on cylinder seals was surely meant to extend the impact of these actions in time. A cylinder with such an image, whether it showed the ruler or some other significant person, must have been considered propitious. One gets the impression that the imagery of the period in Uruk was largely ritual, whereas in Susa it was largely concerned with crafts and other activities necessary for the upkeep of a vast economy. For an example from the latter site one may point to the representation of a loom [Fig. 32] or of a potter's workshop [Fig. 33] among the seal impressions of Susa.

The creation of monsters by seal engravers was another achievement of the period. To the serpo-felines should be added the lion-headed eagle. According to Wiggermann he is the bird of the god of air and wind, Enlil, if represented frontally soaring above other animals. I find very convincing Wiggermann's interpretation of the silver vase of Entemena, [Fig. 34]: the ibexes belong to Enki,[38] the stags to the goddess Ninhursag.[39] These two deities are the divine father and mother of the god Ningirsu to whom the vase is dedicated and whose symbol are the lions.[40]

Here we have arrived at the principal representations of the period following the Uruk age, the Early Dynastic period, ca. 2900–2400 B.C. In the cylinders of that period, which constitute the most numerous works of art, friezes of animals and heroes form the major subject [Fig.35].[41] Scenes of banquets[42] are another motif of which many

Fig. 32. Seal impression from Susa: weavers at a loom (after Amiet, *Glyptique mésopotamienne archaique*, No. 275, pl. 16).

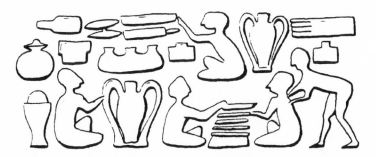

Fig. 33. Seal Impression from Susa: a potter's workshop (after Amiet, *Glyptique mésopotamienne archaique*, pl. 16, no. 265).

examples were found in the graves of the so-called Royal Cemetery of Ur, which we now believe was the burial place of high priestesses of the moon-god Sin.[43] Perhaps the scenes portray the funerary banquets held for the persons buried in the cemetery. One of the most elaborate banqueting scenes was found in the subterranean tomb chamber of "queen", or high priestess, Puabi, formerly called Shubad [Fig. 36]. It is a cylinder of exceptionally fine blue lapis lazuli.

Fig. 34. Silver vase of Entemena (extended drawing after *Reallexikon der Assyriologie und vorderasiatische Archäologie* Bd. 7:1/2, 1987, p. 95, Abb. I).

In the Third Early Dynastic period of about 2550 B.C. the nude bearded hero with six curls was given greater

Fig. 35. Cylinder seal and a modern impression showing contest of bull-man with lions and horned animals, Early Dynastic IIIA, British Museum (after Strommenger, *5000 Years,* Fig. 42c).

distribution in the friezes. This makes his appearance in the later cylinder seals of developed Akkadian style of

Fig. 36. Modern impression of the cylinder seal of Puabi from Ur, Grave 800 (after Strommenger, *5000 Years*, Fig. 64, left, second from top).

about 2200 B.C. [Fig. 37] seem like a natural development of a figure whose frontal face framed by distinctive curls and a nude muscular body made him a likely representative of super-human physical power. He is most often associated with the water buffalo, an animal, perhaps imported from India for the new Semitic ruler of Mesopotamia, Sargon of Akkade.[44] The animal would have certainly been observed by the local population in its enjoyment of bathing in available pools. Its love of water may have strengthened the association of the hero with curls with the god Enki, [Fig. 27] with whom there may have existed the earlier association indicated by the fish hanging from the snake-man's necklace in our Uruk period figure [Fig. 25].

Fig. 37. Hero with curls fighting a water buffalo, bull-man fighting a lion. Modern impression of a cylinder seal, Akkadian, ca. 2200 B.C. The Pierpont Morgan Library, No. 159.

The Akkad period, ca. 2400–2150 B.C., was a period in which the Mesopotamian gods obtained visual form. It is likely that, as Henri Frankfort assumed, the seal cutters were the creators of many of the images, but some were formed earlier. The first deity to be given visual form was Inanna, later the Akkadian Ishtar.

The present cylinder [Fig. 38] was in the collection of the late Mossène Foroughi, a man of exceptional taste and discernement. Here Inanna, with bull-horned crown like all other gods at that period,[45] is shown with the bull of heaven who supports a winged structure.[46] The details of the myth upon which these representations are based are not known. Unlike other goddesses, Inanna is shown with frontal face and here seems to overpower the bull who is seen elsewhere [Fig. 39], lying quietly as a docile adjunct of the goddess who holds the rope by which the gates were pulled open. Nothing is known about the two

Fig. 38. Ishtar dominating a bull who carries a winged structure, gods fighting. Modern impression of a cylinder seal, Akkadian, ca. 2400-2150 B.C. Foroughi Collection.

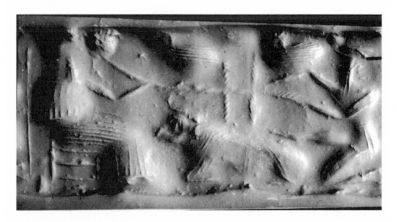

Fig. 39. Ishtar holding the rope of the gate carried by a recumbent bull. Modern impression of a cylinder seal, Akkadian. The Pierpont Morgan Library, No. 226.

Fig. 40. The sun-god Shamash between the wings of the Gate of Heaven. Modern impression of a cylinder seal, Akkadian. Foroughi Collection.

fighting figures on the cylinder [Fig. 38] one of whom has lost his mace and stands with a gesture of utter helplessness. The god who holds the structure also grasps the rope of the gate at the end of which seems to be a pointed metal post, perhaps to anchor the rope when the gate was open.

The gods most frequently represented on the Akkadian cylinders were the water-god Enki-Ea [Figs 1, 2] and the sun-god Shamash, the Sumerian Utu. The sun-god was shown enthroned as in another cylinder originally in the Foroughi Collection [Fig. 40]. He is seen holding up his emblematic saw between the wings of the gate of heaven, which are pulled open by two assistant gods and which are topped by lions whose roar was thought to equal the noise made by the opening of the gates. Before the sun-god stands the double-faced minister Isimud who appears

Fig. 41. Drawing of an Akkad period seal impression from Brak. Courtesy of David and Joan Oates.

elsewhere as the adjunct of the water-god Enki-Ea. A worshiper brings an offering of a young goat and holds a plow; beside him a serpent is drawn vertically in the field. The exchange of the double-faced minister with the water-god is curious, as well as the association of the worshiper with a plow, generally shown with deities of vegetation, while the serpent may point to deities of the netherworld. The cylinder shows the variety which existed between cylinders of a given period made at different locations, for I believe this cylinder to have come from the region of Brak in Syria where similar figures occur on a seal impression of the Akkad period excavated by David and Joan Oates [Fig. 41].[47] In both the Foroughi cylinder and the Brak impression the figures have short upper bodies and long lower ones and in both the iconography does not conform to the majority of the Akkadian seal designs of the subject as assembled by Boehmer (see note 46).

Great efforts were made by the seal cutters of the Akkad

Fig. 42. Weather gods. Modern impression of a cylinder seal, Akkadian. The Pierpont Morgan Library, No. 220.

Fig. 43. Hero with curls and bull-man fighting a lion-griffin. Modern impression of a cylinder seal, Ur III, ca. 2112–2004 B.C. The Pierpont Morgan Library, No. 268.

period to create beautifully engraved scenes in which the gods were shown within their context. Thus the weather-god appears on his chariot with the rain-goddess standing an a monster with the body of a lion but wings, hind feet and a tail of an eagle [Fig. 42]. That monster, whose

Sumerian name is translated as "big weather beast" by Wiggermann[48] but called by me lion-griffin, had already appeared at the end of the third Early Dynastic period.

The lion-griffin, appeared on cylinder seals of the time of the Third Dynasty of Ur (2112–2004 B.C.) as a monster which occasionally replaced the lion as the enemy of heroes [Fig. 43], its pictorial role changed from adjunct of the weather god to enemy of man, and, later, also of gods.

The meaning of the principal scene of cylinders of the Ur III period no longer describes a heroic or other important action of a deity as in most Akkadian cylinders, but the presentation of a worshiper to a deity or to the king, which we will not pursue here.[49]

In Old Babylonian cylinders [Fig. 44] the lion-griffin

Fig. 44. Nude hero with curls grasping a bull-man, lion-griffin menacing a seated goat, kneeling man assailed by a lion. Modern impression of a cylinder seal, Old Babylonian, ca. 19th–18th century B.C. The Pierpont Morgan Library, No. 359.

Fig. 45. Clay plaque with the face of Humbaba, ca. 19-18th century B.C. (after Henri Frankfort, *The Art and Architecture of the Ancient Orient*. 4th rev. impression, Baltimore: Penguin Books, 1970, Fig. 125).

appears as an attacker of the seated goat or of a nude man. The man could be an enemy but the goat is not an aggressive creature. The representations remain enigmatic perhaps reflecting the relations of astral constellations.

Clay plaques representing single figures were found in the levels of the Isin-Larsa and Old Babylonian periods (ca. 2000–1600 B.C.).[50] Unfortunately the precise circumstances of their finds were not recorded. The subject matter is varied: many animal figures and figures of nude

Fig. 46. Ugly head of a demon, early first millennium B.C., Musée du Louvre (photograph by E. Porada).

females were found. Occasionally there are figures known from the contemporary cylinder seals, like the bull-man or the nude bearded hero with curls.[51]

Most significant among the clay plaques of that period is the grinning face of the giant Humbaba [Fig. 45] who was killed by the hero Gilgamesh and his friend Enkidu.[52] It was a mask, so ugly that it would frighten men and demons and prevent them from entering the gate at which it was hung.

I think this is the first example of the carver not being frightened of offending a superhuman power by creating an ugly image of it. However, the really horrible images of powerful demons appeared only in Neo-Assyrian and Neo-Babylonian art in the first millennium B.C. At that time, the artist may have been sufficiently secure in his belief in magical protective texts to give free reign to his imagination of the horrible [Fig. 46].

On the cylinder seals the fearsome features were concentrated on the monster pursued by a god, probably Ninurta [Fig. 47]. This Neo-Babylonian cylinder is another example from the Foroughi Collection, dated about 700 B.C. Another monster, a bull-headed serpent [Fig. 48] seen especially on Assyrian cylinders of a slightly earlier period, the ninth to eighth century B.C., is as yet unidentified, perhaps the personnified sea, enemy of the gods or some other evil creature about to be killed by a heroic god.

We will now turn to the texts used for defense against disease, which was most feared of all the possible disasters because of its unknown causes. I rely on Wiggermann's writings for the following citations.

A house in which there had been illness and other

Fig. 47. A god, probably Ninurta, in an attack on a lion-griffin. Modern impression of a cylinder seal, Neo-Babylonian, ca 700 B.C. Foroughi Collection.

Fig. 48. A god attacking a horned serpent. Modern impression of a cylinder seal, Neo-Assyrian, ninth to eighth century B.C. The Pierpont Morgan Library, No. 688.

disasters was to be cleaned and protected against all types of evil spirits by an extensive ritual.[53] The section of the text concerning the making of statues begins with a heading indicating the subject:

[when you make the statues of *cornel* wood][54]
In the morning at sunrise, you shall go to the wood,
[you shall take] a golden axe and a ⌈silver⌉ saw,
with censer, torch and ⌈holy⌉ water
you shall consecrate
[the *cornel* tree.

later in the text the exorcist is told:

With the golden axe and the silver saw
you shall touch the *cornel* tree and
cut it down with a hatchet.

How factually the ritual describes the action to be taken since the precious implements could not have been used for the task of cutting down a tree!

The ritual implement, the silver saw and doubtless also the golden axe had a long history in Mesopotamian ritual for in the tomb of Puabi, Grave 800 of the Royal Cemetery of Ur, there was a golden saw, as well as in the close vicinity two bronze axes with gold bindings.[55] Silver or gold, it was made of pure and precious material and was surely used for ritual purposes. This may reconfirm Moorey's suggestion that the great dead in the cemetery had been high priestesses of the local god.

Returning to excerpts from Wiggermann's text, seven statues were to be made of pieces of *cornel* wood. Their names were written on their left shoulder. The first statue

Fig. 49. Ishtar, another god, and worshiper. Modern impression of a cylinder seal, Neo-Assyrian, eighth century B.C. Rosen Collection.

Fig. 50. Supernatural defenders of a house or person. Modern impression of a cylinder seal, Neo-Assyrian, eigth century B.C. Buffalo, Museum of Science, 14424.

is clad in red paste for his uniform, the next in white paste and so on through the various colors. The one covered with red paste was called "offspring of Ur," the one with white paste was called "day of plenty, son of Nippur," and so through the major ancient towns of Mesopotamia. Then the exorcist has to make statues of tamarisk wood. Of these, seven statues are of the Sebettu,

> crowned with their own tiara, clad in their own garment, you shall place them on a pedestal of tamarisk in a walking pose; they are clad in red paste over their uniform; hold in their right hands a hatchet of bronze and in their left ⌈hands⌉ a dagger of bronze and are bound around their waist with a ⌈girdle⌉ of bronze and around their heads with a ⌈headband⌉ of bronze, furnished with ⌈horn⌉s of bronze, and bows and quivers hang at their sides.

We may imagine that they were thought to look much like the representations of Ishtar on Neo-Assyrian hard stone cylinder seals [Fig. 49]. One such cylinder in the Buffalo Museum of Science [Fig. 50] may well represent such a group of semi-divine defenders.

More statues of gods and warriors for the defense of the house and its owners were to be carved of tamarisk wood. They and minor figures, like fishmen, or monsters and dogs made of clay were to be buried at the outer gate of the house and at specifically indicated places throughout the house. The wooden images were not preserved but some of the clay ones were found. Of course, they are crude, like the fishman [Fig. 51]. But the image in the mind of the Assyrian user was the one known from art, as

Fig. 51. Terracotta figurine: fish-man (after Dessa Rittig, *Assyrisch Babylonische Kleinplastik magischer Bedeutung vom. 13. - 6. Jh. v. Chr.* Munchen: Verlag Uni-Druck, 1977, pl. 32).

Fig. 52. Fishmen flanking a sacred tree and hero attacking an ostrich. Modern impression of a cylinder seal, Neo-Assyrian, late eighth century B.C. The Pierpont Morgan Library, No. 773.

I implied with the image of Ishtar. The same may be said of the stately finely engraved fishmen shown on a Neo-Assyrian cylinder seal [Fig. 52]. Likewise, the image of the hero on that cylinder gives us some idea of the manner in which the heroic defenders of the endangered house would have appeared in the imagination of its inhabitants.

The protection of a person or an entire family was not the only duty of the figurines created by the relevant priests. The Babylonians were able to protect themselves against a disaster which had been predicted for them. All sorts of omina served to warn them of such events; the behavior of animals, human beings, plants, the movements of the stars, the weather, all could indicate propitious or unfavorable events. Knowing what the future might bring, there could have been found some means to avoid the disaster in the extensive collections of rituals. Stefan Maul[56] gives the following example: if a dog in the house of a man howls continuously this means bad luck for the houseowner and his family. However, it is not only a sign of bad luck, it was sent by the man's personal gods because they were annoyed for some reason and wanted to punish him. The dog represents the danger threatening the man. The ritual preventing the disaster had the following points: the man had to assuage the wrath of the gods; the man had to succeed in making the gods change their resolution to decree an unfavorable destiny for him; the uncleanliness which the man and his surroundings had caught had to be eliminated. The man had to be introduced again to his normal living conditions. The man had to be provided with lasting protection against further disastrous omina. The god particularly involved was Shamash, the protector and guardian of creation who was to lead the man back into the right ways. Before the beginning of the ritual, the dog which had howled had to be caught, or a figure of the dog made. At the divine hearing the man had to raise the dog figure to Shamash and the conjurer defended the man and accused the clay animal of all the sins and transgressions of which the man might have been guilty.

For us the important part is the elimination of the dog figure, representing the creature that had indicated the bad omen. We may assume that it looked like other clay figures of dogs though these were made for a different, protective purpose. The conjurer and the man went together to the bank of the river with sacrifices for the river. Then they spoke the words of the ritual "Thou, river, pull down the dog to the *apsu*." Then the conjurer threw the dog figure into the river. Since it certainly sank, as would have been the case in guilty persons, the guilt of the omen indicator was proven.

The most extensive rituals were those devised against the child snatching Lamashtu, the worst demon of Assyro-Babylonian religion, whose influence reached to

Fig. 53, 54. Bronze Lamashtu amulet, early first millennium B.C. Formerly in the De Clercq Collection, now Paris, Musée du Louvre.

central Asia as well as to Greece.[57] Reliefs representing the horrible demon were carved and probably hung at the entrance of habitations. She has certain Elamite associations though she is integrated into the Mesopotamian pantheon as the daughter of the sky god Anu and as

having been given a lion's or dog's head by the god Enlil. The earliest descriptions of Lamashtu date from the Akkadian period but the so-called canonical texts' descriptions of Lamashtu and rituals to be recited derive from the second quarter of the first millennium B.C. Reliefs showing the demon tell her story.

The great amulet from the former De Clercq Collection [Fig. 53/54] shows in the top row a series of symbols of the great gods. In the second register is a row of animal headed demons whose role is not defined. In the third register are the fish-apkallu. Apkallu are the wise men of Babylonian prehistory who devised the medicines to heal the sick. They flank the bed of the sick person beside which is the lamp of the god of light, Nusku. The lion-headed, war-like demons were probably intended to prevent the return of Lamashtu who appears in the lowest register, kneeling on a donkey with a dog and a piglet at her pendant nude breasts. In her hands she holds serpents. In the right corner are the gifts that were to entice Lamashtu to depart: the objects which are clearly recognizable are a small oil jar, a comb, a fibula, the leg of a donkey, and a piece of textile.

Once a conjurer-priest has determined that the patient has been attacked by Lamashtu he enters upon a long procedure of rituals. Again I rely on Wiggermann's writings.[58] On the first day he makes an image of Lamashtu as a prisoner, he pours water before her, provides her with a few gifts and puts the heart of a piglet in her mouth. It is hoped that she will be transformed into a black dog. In the hope that she has gone into her image it is taken out and buried at the city wall.

On the fourth day the priest makes an image of her, robes her, gives her a comb, a spindle and a small jar of oil. These gifts are to tempt her away from the patient and encourage her to depart on a trip.

On the following day the priest takes the image and the traveling equipment into the steppe and turns the image's head to the east. In the conjurations the demon is encouraged to travel across the Ulai, a river in Elam. On the sixth day the priest makes an image of DIM.ME the Sumerian name of Lamashtu and places it beside a pot in which there is a dagger. These are to be placed next to the head of the patient.

A helper in the fight against Lamashtu is Pazuzu, a wind demon,[59] who appears beside Lamashtu on the relief and also looks over the relief and seems to hold it up if seen

Fig. 55.
The demon,
Pazuzu,
Paris, Musée
du Louvre,
Photo by
Edith
Porada.

from the back. These are truly horrible images thought to represent the monster itself, who would be so frightened by the sight of his own appearance that he would flee [Fig. 55].

Viewing the images here shown and the texts that explain them, we realize that the omina that served to warn the Assyrians and Babylonians of unfavorable future events were not proof of "a terrible superstition" as stated by Bruno Meissner in *Babylonien und Assyrien,* 1925, p. 198,[60] but instead, it gave these people a sense of security. The security was based on the trust in the exorcists, the "men of science" of the day who had libraries of protective rituals at their disposition.

The biblical writers, however, would have seen the exorcists' provisions for the future as an incursion into the realm of the Almighty. And from this viewpoint we also understand more fully the interdiction of the third commandment to Moses and the people: "Thou shalt not make thee any graven images[61] or any likeness of anything that is in heaven or that is in the earth beneath, or that is in the water beneath the earth." For to make such images, was to create beings with a reality of their own[62] [Fig. 56] and in that belief, shared by the makers and their recipients, lies the source of the intensity of ancient Near Eastern art.

Fig. 56. Goat-
man, ca. 3000 B.C.,
on loan from
Robin B. Martin
to the Brooklyn
Musuem.

# DISCUSSION

F.A.M. WIGGERMANN
*Extensions of and Contradictions
to Dr. Porada's Lecture*

First I want to express my gratitude to Dr. Anshen and Dr. Ryskamp for having invited me to the Frick Collection, and to Dr. Porada for giving me the opportunity to "provide extensions of or contradictions to" her text. I will center my comments on the empirical bases of our interpretations of Mesopotamian art, and discuss a number of examples that, I hope, illustrate not only my points, but also throw light from a different angle on Dr. Porada's expert exposition.

Mesopotamian art, unlike its Egyptian and Greek counterparts, is hardly ever provided with captions or explanatory text. Captions identifying the symbols of gods occur occasionally on boundary stones (*kudurrus*), one of which will be shown later. Other supernatural figures and divine symbols can be identified by matching texts that describe or mention them with the actual images. The two most important texts of this type, the one treating the defense of a house against intruding evil and the one providing protection against the baby-snatching she-demon Lamaštu, were extensively quoted by Dr. Porada. Notwithstanding the importance of these texts, their coverage is far from complete, and many symbols and figures of the long history of Mesopotamian art remain nameless and of uncertain meaning.

The interpretation of the scenes in which the figures and symbols occur is no less difficult, and often lacks a firm footing in the texts. Contrary to Greek art, where most of the scenes can be interpreted by linking them to

Fig. 57. Gods toiling before the creation of humanity. Drawing of a modern impression of a cylinder seal, Akkadian, ca. 2200 B.C. (after Opitz, Tf. III, Fig. 58, see my text, note 1).

well known stories about gods and heroes, Mesopotamian art hardly ever takes its material directly from narrative literature. Literature and art centre on the same basic issues of theology, but each in its own way: man serving his gods; heroes, gods or kings defending him against human and demonic enemies; the relations between the members of the pantheon. An exceptionally detailed match between text and image is provided by a late third millennium B.C. Akkadian seal [Fig. 57][1] illustrating the sequence of events leading up to the creation of humanity. An early second millennium B.C. myth[2] relating these events begins: "when the gods like men bore the work and carried the basket". On the seal the gods are building a temple, one is carrying the basket, while another is mixing mortar with a hoe. Basket and hoe are the proverbial tools of hard labor, and the myth continues to tell how much the toiling gods suffered until they decided to stand up against their masters, the seven great gods, and to go on strike. The great gods kill their leader, but take pity on the toiling gods and from his flesh and blood mixed with clay create a substitute, man. From then on *he* carries the basket (Figs. 3a and b). The seal further shows a god being killed by a "great" god, and a second "great" god in the attitude of an atlant. His identity is uncertain, but he may well be Enlil, "Lord Ether", the leader of the great gods, who, by his very existence, holds heaven and earth separated.[3]

Such detailed correspondances are rare,[4] and in most cases the modern scholar has to recreate the ideas that inform the imagery from scattered bits and pieces found in the written and visual sources of three millennia of Mesopotamian civilization. This process can be demonstrated by a brief analysis of a late Early Dynastic document found in one of the graves of the so-called Royal

Fig. 58. Inlaid panel of Lyre: Scene from the Other Side, animals making music and preparing a banquet. Early Dynastic IIIA, ca. 2500 B.C., from grave PG 789, Ur (after Orthmann, Pl. IX, see my text, note 5).

Cemetery at Ur, being the front panel of a lyre [Fig. 58].[5] The lower register is the smallest, and therefore probably the least important, which indicates that, as more often, the monument has to be read from bottom to top. The contents of the lower register support this way of reading: the scorpion-man (*Girtablullû*) is known from the Epic of Gilgamesh to guard the mythical mount Twin-Peaks (*Māšu*), the entrance to the Other Side. I quote the text from Maureen Gallery Kovacs's translation:

When he (Gilgamesh) reached Mount Twin-Peaks,
which daily guards the rising and setting of the Sun,
whose top [touches] the dome of heaven,
and whose flank reaches as far as the Netherworld below,

> there were Scorpion-Beings watching over its gate.
> Trembling terror they inspire, the sight of them is death,
> their aweful radiance (*melammu*) sweeps over the mountains.
> At the rising and setting they watch over the Sun.
> When Gilgamesh saw them, trembling terror blanketed his face,
> but he pulled himself together and drew near to them.

The scorpion-man, who does not normally meet mortals, concludes that his visitor must be a god, but his wife corrects him: "(Only) two-thirds of him is a god, one-third is human".[6]

A late Babylonian document known as the *Map of the World* locates the mythical scorpion-man and other monsters at the edge of the earth, together with a series of wild animals: mountain goat, gazelle, water-buffalo, panther, lion, wolf, red-dear, hyena, monkey, she-monkey, ibex, ostrich, cat, and chameleon. They are associated in some way (the text is broken at this point) with the flood-hero Ut-Napištim, the legendary conquerer of distant lands Sargon, and with beings supplied with wings.[7] Towards the edges of the earth reality loses its grip and shifts into the wild, wondrous, monstrous, and primeval. It is to these regions that the dead go after they have crossed the desert and the Other World river Ḫubur.

Elements of this Other World imagery occur in various combinations on seals and other works of art from the Early Dynastic period onwards. Although much material remains to be analyzed, it might be suggested that contest scenes involving the nude hero with curls (*laḫmu*), the bull-man (*kusarikku*), and wild animals take place in this Other World (Fig. 37). Regularly such scenes are set in a mountainous environment, definitively not the Meso-potamian plains.

The Other World, located at the mountains of sun-set and sun-rise, is supervised by the sun-god (Utu/Šamaš) who daily travels the expanse of the universe and is known as the "sheikh of the Big City"[8] where he judges the dead. He is narrowly associated with a number of peripheral monsters, such as the scorpion-man, the bull-man, and the human-faced bull. The static, emblematic scene in the top register of the panel, two human-faced bulls mastered by a nude hero, contrasts with the action of the other registers, and signifies the dominion of the sun-god.

The two middle registers show animals making music and preparing a banquet: a hyena (?) carrying a serving table on which are a lamb's head, a boar's head and a leg of mutton; a lion with a large vessel and in his right hand a cup or a lamp; a bear clapping and dancing; a small animal playing a sistrum, on its knees a small drum; and an ass singing and playing the lyre. Clearly these animals stand outside the normal order, just as the scorpion-man and the human-faced bull they are associated with. As indicated by other works of art and the *Map of the World*, they are inhabitant of the periphery, where nature gets a diabolical twist.

The object of which the panel under discussion forms part is a lyre with a bull-shaped body, the same type of lyre as the one being played by the ass. It may not be stretching the imagination too much to conclude that with this self-reference the panel reveals the purpose of the object it forms part of: it will serve at a banquet similar to the one depicted on the panel, a feast to be held at the Other Side. The expected guest, so conspiciously absent on the panel, is the person laid to rest in the grave where the lyre was found, and the lyre is among his gifts to the inhabitants of the Other Side, the world of the dead. Although elements of the imagery occur elsewhere, the whole configuration is unique, and it may be concluded that the lyre was commissioned precisely for the occasion of this specific burial.

Medieval western parallels were discussed by Wilhelm Stauder in 1969.[9] The most interesting one stems from a capital of the 12th century on the Palacio de los Reyes de Navarra in the Spanish town of Estella. It shows a seated ass playing the lyre, and devils cooking the souls of sinners in a large cauldron, and obviously aims at inspiring the believers with fear for hell. It is not known along which channels this diabolical ass reached the West.

The ass playing the lyre leads us to another source of doubt concerning the possibility of fully understanding Mesopotamian art: the use of allegory. That abstract notions may lurk behind the scenes is demonstrated by a text dating to the second half of the second millennium B.C., the *Description of Gods* better known under its German name as the *Göttertypentext*.[10] The text describes in detail twenty-seven images of gods and monsters, their headdresses, hairdoes, clothing, attributes, and postures. Since the images often deviate from what is known to be normal, the text cannot be used for straightforward identifications. The iconographic program it implies is unique, and may never have been executed. Even so, the text reveals an unexpected inclination to visualize abstractions as acting beings. It personifies four nouns that are not personified anywhere else, and represents them as monsters: Conflict (*adammû*) and Struggle (*ippiru*) grasping each other, Zeal (*ḫinṭu*) and Grief (*niziqtu*). That the beings are monsters is quite in accordance with their unpleasant character, but the detailed descriptions specify images that are not actually attested in the long history of Mesopotamian art, showing that they were invented to match the freshly created demonic abstractions. I quote the description of Grief:

> the head is supplied with a cap and horns of an ox; he is supplied with ears of an ox; the hair hangs loose over his back; the face is that of a woman; his hands are those of a man; he is supplied with wings and his (text: her) hands are stretched out towards (?) his (text: her) wings; the naked body is that of a woman; his feet stand in the *ḫuppu* (unknown) posture.

The monstrous abstractions of the *Göttertypentext* open our eyes to the possibility that the actually attested actors of Mesopotamian art may have had such abstract connotations as well, which is, in fact, confirmed by other texts.[11] In this context I want to view the battles between gods so often found on Akkadian seals. Above, in connection with the creation of man, we interpreted one of these battles as the execution of the rebellious foreman of the working gods. From the texts we know that historical wars against mountain peoples were sometimes cast in the form of a hymnic myth, with Mesopotamian gods in the role of victor, and a rebellious mountain god as the vanquished enemy. Inanna's victory over mount Ebih, the

Fig. 59. Rebel gods being defeated. Drawing of a modern impression of a cylinder seal. Akkadian, ca. 2200 B.C. (after Sotheby's London, Monday 10th July 1989, *Antiquities from the Schuster Collection*, no. 20).

ancient name of the Himrin chain separating the low-lands from the Iranian mountains, is generally considered to be such mythological history.[12] In a more general way the god Ninurta, the warrior of his father Enlil, plays the part of subduer of the mountains and victor over a whole series of monstrous enemies. On Akkadian seals his place is taken by the young hero Šamaš, the sun-god, some-times assisted by his sister Inanna. The rebel gods they defeat may be identified by a small mountain on which they recline while dying, but generally remain feature-less, so that they can hardly be interpreted as the specific enemies of specific occasions, whether mythological or historical. I do not think that the fiery rays that sometimes emanate from their shoulders or from the mountain they recline on[13] establish them as gods of light, fire, or heat; it is rather their "aweful radiance" (*melammu*)[14] that we saw "sweep over the mountains" in the case of the scorpion-men[15] encountered above [Fig. 58]. The broken mace or the mace slipped from his hand aptly symbolizes the end of the rebel's power. Thus, when context or attributes do not identify the vanquished god, the battle scene does not refer to a specific mythological occasion but denotes in a general manner the ascendancy of the gods of civilization over their foreign enemies; it is the ancient equivalent of the text that adorns European coins: god be with us.[16]

Similar problems are encountered in the interpretation of the parts played by animals in the symbolism of ancient Mesopotamian art. In the historical periods most symbolic animals were integrated into the iconography of the anthropomorphic gods, to whom they may be related in a variety of ways. In the prehistoric periods, before the reorganization of religion that took place concomitantly with the rise of the first states, the animals may have been some kind of spirits with properties similar to those of their later anthropomorphic masters.[17] Thus, for example, the scorpion-man, an acolyte of the sun-god, is demonstrably derived from a cosmic scorpion that with its pinchers moves the stars through heaven.[18] At the same time the scorpion symbolizes carnal love.[19] As we saw above in connection with the *Map of the World*, wild animals, in the later periods sometimes supplied with wings, may embody the eerie periphery and as such appear as the enemies of (the gods of) civilization (Fig. 50).

One source for the early history of animal symbolism is

nearly universally ignored: the names of the stars and constellations. Undoubtedly some of them were named on the basis of a prehistoric or early historic agricultural calender, but since most of our astrological sources stem from the first millennium B.C., the original symbolism is extremely hard to reconstruct.[20] There may be other motives too, however. Thus we encounter the scorpion again as a constellation, identified by the Babylonians themselves as the love goddess Išhara.[21] The Greeks use the same name for this group of stars, and Hans Georg Gundel[22] suggested that it is a "natural constellation which was named in prehistory". According to Greek lore, preserved by Aratus (*Phaenomena* 634ff.)[23] and considered old by Gundel, the hunter Orion, one of the few constellations known by Homer (*Illiad* 18:485ff.), "flees at the western verge at the rising of the Scorpion in the East". This scorpion has nothing to do with love, but is simply the natural enemy of the hunter at the opposite side of heaven. The Mesopotamians too have a human figure opposite the Scorpion, which, however, they have named in accordance with their pastoralist nature the "True Shepherd of Heaven" (*Sipazianna*). This seems to indicate that like the Greeks the earlier Mesopotamians viewed the heavenly scorpion as an enemy of man, rather than as the symbolic presence of the goddess of love.

Slightly altered and translated into Greek and Latin many of the Mesopotamian constellations, whether natural or not, are preserved in western sources from the fourth century B.C. onwards.[24] A good example is Capricorn, whom we will encounter below.

From the fifth millennium B.C. onwards the ibex is prominently present in Mesopotamian iconography, and it is known that at least in the second half of the third it was associated with Enki/Ea, the god of sweet water, wisdom, and male sexuality. It is not known what aspect of the god the animal represents nor if it could be associated with some other god. The fourth millen-

Fig. 60. Temple front and ibex-god. Drawing of double-sided stamp seal, Late Ubaid (?), fourth millennium B.C. (after P. Amiet, "L'Iconographie archaïque de l'Iran," *Syria* 56, 1976, p. 338, Fig. 14).

nium B.C. witnesses a remarkable development, the combination of a human body with an ibex head (Fig. 21),[25] a type of figure that died out again in the third millennium B.C. From a long series of examples it can reasonably be concluded that the ibex-human composite was a Master-of-the-Animals type of god, a superhuman protector of human and animal life. A square stamp seal of unknown but possibly Iranian provenance [Fig. 60][26] with an ibex-god on one side and a temple front on the other indicates that he was in some way connected with a cult. A further development took place in Susa, where during this period a temple-state was established, organized along the same lines as the somewhat later Mesopotamian ones (Susa I).[27] Essential for this type of state is the coincidence of wordly and spiritual power in a temple-annex-storehouse that receives, records, and redistributes the production of a sizeable part of the population. The Susanian ibex-god (Fig. 20) wears a skirt, of which on the present example only the band around the waist is visible.[28] Most interesting is the round object on his breast, which, as Dr. Porada suggests, may be a large stamp seal with a special representation worn as an emblem of distinction. The distinction conveyed by a stamp seal must have to do with its sealing capacity, with the opening and closing of the sealed doors of the storerooms, or, in other words, with the redistributive economy of the temple-state. Wondering what the "special representation" on this stamp seal might have been, we may go one step further and suggest that it was the very special representation that we see before us, the ibex-god mastering snakes, and that by this self-reference the image explains its meaning: the ibex-god wears a seal with his own image, which defines him as the top figure in the redistributive hierarchy. In fact this is exactly what we find somewhat later in Mesopotamia, where the god is the head of state, the temple his residence, and the human priest-king his first servant, the one who actually

receives and redistributes. With a seal such as the one
under discussion the actual power of the redistributive
elite headed by the priest-king is derived from the religious weight of their divine master, the head of state.
Thus, in our view, the Susanian ibex-god constitutes a
special development, an adaptation of a preexisting god
to the requirements of the growing state. It is interesting
to note that the Mesopotamian god Enki/Ea, the later
master of the ibex, has, under his local name Ḥaja, a
similar function: he owns a seal[29] and is married to the
grain goddess Nisaba, who is also the goddess of writing
and administration.

The Susanian ibex-god mastering snakes is matched by
a human figure wearing a cap with ibex horns and
mastering lions.[30] It is a reasonable guess that he is the
priest-king who with his horned mitre indicates his
affiliation to the ibex-god. In this light I want to view the
copper figures from Brooklyn [Figs. 9, 11] and Buffalo in
whose bird features Dr. Porada detects elements of a
shamanistic past, although, as she says, their meaning
may have changed in the Uruk period. To the description
I would like to add that he is lifting his right heel, that he
is making a step, a unique feature that, coupled to the
remarkable shoes, is an important clue for any interpretation. Dr. Porada suggests "magically speedy advance",
but I see steady progress and was reminded of the legendary royal travellers of the early third millennium B.C.,
Enmerkar, Lugalbanda, and ultimately also Gilgamesh.[31]

Finally the ibex of Enki/Ea leads to the ram-god
Mummu, another animal of Enki/Ea with whom I want to
conclude. The identity of the ram-god as Mummu is

established by the inscriptions and captions on boundary stones.[32] On this example [Fig. 61] we see a whole series of divine symbols, the heavenly bodies Sun, Moon, and Venus, the lamp-god Nusku, and others among which the head of Ea's ram Mummu, resting on his temple, which in its turn rests on his goat-fish (*Suḫurmašu*). This goat-fish is the constellation Capricorn, which in Greece, Rome [Fig. 62] and the medieval West was still rendered as a goat-fish. Since the goat-fish does not play any part in Greek mythology or art,[33] it is certain that this image was borrowed from the Babylonians. In the cosmogony of the

Fig. 61 Boundary stone: divine symbols with captions. Middle Babylonian, late second millennium B.C., from Susa (drawing after J. de Morgan, *Mémoires de la Délégation en Perse* I 167ff, 168 Abb. 379. Cf. U. Seidl, "Die babylonische Kudurru-Reliefs," *Baghdader Mitteilungen* 4, 1986, no. 29).

F.A.M. WIGGERMANN

Fig. 62 Roman coin: the constellation Capricorn. Time of Augustus (drawing after W. Kenton, *Astrology. The Celestial Mirror,* 1974, 1991, p. 101, Fig. 11; see also H. G. Gundel, *Zodiakos. Tierkreisbilder im Altertum,* Mainz, 1992, passim).

Babylonian Creation-Myth (*Enūma Eliš*) Mummu is the audible manifestation of the primeval waters (*Apsŭ*).[34] Many centuries later, around 480 of our age, the neoplatonian philosopher Damascius comments on this god in his book "On First Principles" (*Peri Archōn*) and explains him as the *noētos kosmos,* the knowable world.[35] It is a salutary thought that in origin his name is nothing more than the bleating of the ram-god: *mu-mu.*[36]

# PERSONAL STATEMENT

EDITH PORADA
*A Personal Account of Understanding
Ancient Near Eastern Art*

In writing a personal statement about my career in the
field of ancient Near Eastern art, I will relate how my own
studies progressed over half a century and explain my
current views on some masterpieces from Mesopotamia.
In discussing these artifacts I will cite the views and
reactions of the early art historians who were the first to
comment on great works of ancient Near Eastern art that
were being revealed in the excavations. I do so because I
want to draw attention to the work and insights of these
previous generations of art historians and to show how
each generation builds on the achievements of its predecessors.

For as long as I can remember, whether it was in the

townhouse in Vienna or in my father's hunting lodge in the summers, I have liked things that could tell me something about their past, like petrified shells or stones.

In Vienna archaeology is under one's feet. The camp of emperor Marcus Aurelius was in what is now the center of town; and—much to the annoyance of the local taxi industry—excavations of Roman buildings are being carried out at present on the Michaeler Platz, a major thoroughfare in the inner city. My father encouraged my archaeological interests and for my tenth birthday gave me a mammoth's tooth, one of several that had been found in the coal mines on whose administrative council he served.

While I was still in the Gymnasium, which in central Europe corresponds to the U. S. high school, the International meeting of Orientalists, which takes place in a different European town every four years, was held in Vienna. A distant cousin of my mother, a professor of Arabic literature, came from Germany to attend this congress and suggested that I come along to some of the lectures. The one I remember was by Ernst Herzfeld, who reported on the excavation by Max Baron Oppenheim at the site of Tell Halaf in northern Syria. At that site was found pottery of what we now know was from the fifth millennium B.C., as well as carved reliefs of the early first millennium B.C., though the latter may have been made somewhat earlier. Herzfeld insisted that both reliefs and pottery were of the fourth millennium B.C., as early as scholars were then willing to place objects which showed some technical skill. This aroused a violent debate, and I still see some of the bearded gentlemen walking out of the hall, shaking their heads and expressing doubts about Herzfeld's sanity.

I had lunch with my cousin, the Egyptologist Wilhelm von Bissing, and a third scholar whose name I cannot recall. At that luncheon my future was determined. The cousin, who had been informed by the family that I wanted to study archaeology, asked in which area I was planning to concentrate. "Crete and Myceanae," I radiantly answered. "Out of the question," thundered the cousin. "That field is overrun. You will study the ancient Near East. Your professor will be Victor Christian."

I did exactly as I was told and went to see Professor Christian after I had finished the Gymnasium. Christian was even more precise than my cousin. He told me then and there that I would be working on seals of the Akkad period (ca. 2340–2150 B.C.), especially since the cousin's sister had a collection of ancient Near Eastern seals, dating from the third to the first millennium B.C. As I think this over, it seems to me that there must have been some collusion, those sixty years ago, among the professors, who all knew one another as we, the professors in Near Eastern Studies in various countries, know one another now. They had decided that a young, eager student was needed to work on the most abundant material of ancient Near Eastern art, the engraved seal stones, specifically on those which showed the most interesting representations, the cylinder seals of the dynasty of Akkad. Today my only regret is that I cannot start again on what is still the most interesting field, still waiting to be fully explored and understood.

Later, my background of a knowledge of seals was to

enable me to undertake the catalogue of the collection of the Pierpont Morgan Library at the request of Belle da Costa Greene, the first director of the Library. As I prepared the case for the 1991 exhibition of masterpieces in the Pierpont Morgan Library, a few weeks ago, I gratefully thought of Miss Greene who entrusted in 1946 to a young, unknown foreigner the work on the then greatest and finest private collection of cylinder seals, paralleled only by the British Museum and the Louvre. I was quite conscious then of the fact that such generous faith in an untried young scholar was possible only in the United States—and this I still believe.

At the University of Vienna, where I studied for five years, from 1930 to 1935, Victor Christian taught Sumerian and Akkadian. It was a foregone conclusion that I would have to study the languages, though my memory is better for pictures than words. Sumerian is called an agglutinative language in which various elements of both meaning and grammatical relations are strung together.

Writing may have been invented to serve Sumerian, though some scholars believe that an earlier language underlies the development of writing. If this were the case, writing was certainly modified at a subsequent stage to serve Sumerian. At first, single pictorial forms constituted the majority of the signs. The meaning of the pictorial form was expressed by words whose sounds were later used as syllables in writing abstract concepts. No change in the radicals of a Sumerian word expressed a concept of time. Specifications like time or person could only be indicated with prefixes or suffixes.

This basic structure of writing and language has always

Fig. 63. Fragment of a limestone votive plaque of Eannatum I or II of Lagash, ca. 2450 B.C., British Museum (after Strommenger, *5000 Years,* Pl. 71).

impressed me as a parallel to the structure of early Mesopotamian art. In Fig. 63, characteristic elements of the human head—its outline, its nose, eye, ear, lips, and chin—each have their own distinctive form which is added to the others to create the timeless head of the ruler of Lagash, Eannatum (I or II), dated approximately 2450 B.C.

Akkadian, the second major language used in Mesopotamia, belongs to the family of Semitic languages,
which seems to have a structure in which the basic
elements are roots of three consonants that are manipu-
lated by additions, doubling, and vowels to give rise to a
vast number of derivative words in various tenses. The
most dramatic representation of the ancient Near East, the
stele of Naram-Sin in the Louvre [Fig. 64] appears to
parallel the flexibility and the vitality of the Akkadian
language.

Christian had a strong interest in archaeology and gave
at least one course in that field in which he presented the
available material, which he had carefully collected from
the few publications of excavations available during my
years of study in Vienna.

Excavations had started shortly before the middle of
the nineteenth century at the Assyrian palaces of Nimrud,
Khorsabad, and Nineveh, dated between ca. 880 B.C. and
the destruction of Nineveh in 612 B.C. They brought to the
images of the Assyrians from the accounts of the Old
Testament and the Greek historians the reality of the
reliefs created by the Assyrians who were responsible for
the military installations, the battles, and the rituals and
processions of the empire and its peoples.

With some gaps in the sequence of excavations as the
result of financial and political limitations there was a
continuation of expeditions to Mesopotamia by the
Americans (Pennsylvania University, 1888–1898) to Nippur, by the French (1877–1933) to Tello (then thought to
have been the town of Lagash, now known to have been

Fig. 64. Limestone victory stele of Naram-Sin, King of Akkad, ca. 2254-2218 B.C., Louvre (after Strommenger *5000 Years*, Pl. 122).

the sanctuary site of Girsu), and by the Germans at Babylon (1899–1917) and Assur.

General interest in the excavated material of the texts, written in cuneiform on stone slabs and clay tablets, was far greater than in the statuary, reliefs, and seals that were being excavated. The connection, actual or imagined, of the texts with those of the Old Testament—for example, an epic that contains elements of the deluge story— doubtless accounted for this widespread interest, which extended even to Gilbert and Sullivan who had the major general in their *Pirates of Penzance* say, "I can write a washing bill in cuneiform."

The early history and evaluation of ancient Mesopotamian art were the work of scholars who had been trained in Greek art. Three individuals stand out, the first, Léon Alexandre Heuzey, had been in excavations in Macedonia and had written on Greek statuary and terra-cottas. He devised an initial chronology of Mesopotamian art on the basis of the rather cursory French excavation reports of the site of Tello in southern Iraq in the book on which he collaborated with Ernest de Sarzec. In a book entitled "the oriental origins of art" he reproduced side by side an Egyptian slate palette and a cylinder seal of about 3000 B.C. Both showing monsters consisting of lion's bodies and serpent necks to illustrate the relation of these early cultures. This relation has only been confirmed in the past two years on the basis of remains of typically Mesopotamian architectural painted cones which were found at Buto in the Nile delta. Heuzey's pioneering work was followed by two significant commentaries on the art of the ancient Near East, both appended to a far larger section on the art of Egypt: Walter Andrae's, "Die Kunst Vorderasiens," which followed Heinrich Schäfer's, "Die Kunst Ägyptens," and Ludwig Curtius's, "Vorderasien."

Andrae's was a very personal account, informed by his intimate knowledge of the countries that produced ancient Near Eastern art. His gradual approach to this art is interesting to observe. In speaking about one of his early excavations in Mesopotamia, he described his pleasure at finding a Hellenistic looking object among all the foreign-looking ones that were being turned up. The Hellenistic object was immediately intelligible to his Greek-trained eye, whereas at that stage in his career the ancient Mesopotamian works seemed dark and foreign.

Influenced by Heuzey's general chronological indications, Andrae divided the Mesopotamian material into an early period of the fourth millennium B.C., and followed by the works of the Akkad and Gudea periods, which he called the golden age of Mesopotamia, and dated them in the middle of the third millennium B.C. These dates are several hundred years earlier than the present datings whereas the dates for the late period in Babylonia and Assyria, the late second and early first millennium B.C., were much as those now accepted.

Andrae recognized fine pottery as the artistic manifestation of the early period of course not realizing the differences in time between the fifth millennium B.C. pottery of Halaf and that of the fourth millennium B.C. one of Susa I, which he considered the finest.

When he wrote his essay he thought that the earliest period known to him had no real architecture, that in the early third millennium B.C. there were only reed huts. But he lived to learn of the magnificent temples built at Uruk Warka five hundred years earlier. One of Andrae's observations was the importance of the central courtyard around which rooms were built, an arrangement which lasted until the late Assyrian period. The main room lay on the south side. The oldest bricks known to Andrae were plano-convex, now known to have been introduced about 2900 B.C. after different types were used in earlier periods.

Andrae saw the height of Mesopotamian art in the period of the Akkad Dynasty, represented by the stele of Naram-Sin, discovered at Susa, where it had been taken as booty from the sun-god's center of Sippar in Babylonia. He also knew several of the magnificent cylinder seals of the period to which Joachim Ménant had drawn attention in one of the first books that used photographic reproductions for ancient Near Eastern cylinder seal impressions.

Andrae linked the sculptures of Gudea, ca. 2150 [Fig. 65], with those of the period of the Akkad Dynasty, ca. 2340–2150 B.C., in the Golden Age of Mesopotamia. The last work included by Andrae in his Golden Age was the stele of Hammurabi [Fig. 66], of which he lauded the naturalism and precise rendering of the figures' profile views.

Andrae's suggestion of the existence of goldsmiths' work in the late period, for which he had very little factual proof but for which he assumed an international guild, reads almost like a presentiment of the gold treasures found in 1989 and 1990 by the Iraqi Antiquities Service in the tombs of Assyrian queens at Nimrud [Fig. 67].

Fig. 65. Statue of Gudea, Ensi of Lagash, ca. 2150-2110 B.C., Louvre (after Strommenger *5000 Years*, Pl. 131).

Fig. 66. Relief from the top of the stele of the Code of Hammurabi, King of Babylon, ca. 1792-1750 B.C., Louvre (after Strommenger *5000 Years*, Pl. 159).

In the discussion of the Assyrian reliefs Andrae showed his sensitive reaction to ancient Near Eastern art in his appreciation of the reliefs of Ashurnasirpal II (883–859 B.C.) [Fig. 68]. He spoke of the massive fullness of the figures, which never appear fat and mushy. He called it a style comparable only with the works of Michelangelo. Andrae devoted great care and understanding to the Late Hittite and Aramaean reliefs and sculptures in the round. By the time that he wrote about these works he had fully accepted the aesthetics of ancient Near Eastern art.

Fig. 67. Jewellery from Nimrud (after *Time*, Oct. 30, 1989, p. 80).

In contrast with Andrae who was primarily an architect and may be said to have influenced the predominance of architecture in German archaeology, Ludwig Curtius was a historian of Greek and Roman art. His searching analysis of Egyptian and Western Asiatic art was sparked by his desire to learn about the foreign influences on Greek art in the eighth and seventh centuries B.C. He therefore made a thorough study of the Assyrian reliefs, especially of the battle and hunting scenes, in which he made important statements about the pictorial structure of the representations.

Fig. 68. Detail from a relief of Ashurnasirpal II, King of Assyria, 883-859 B.C., Metropolitan Museum of Art.

Among the reliefs he chose for reproduction in *Antike Kunst* was one from the series in the throne room of the palace of Ashurnasirpal II at Nimrud-Kalah which shows fugitives swimming toward a city surrounded by water and identified by Irene J. Winter as Carchemish [Fig. 69]. Curtius described the relief as showing a unified perspective with a high viewpoint. He drew attention to the manner in which the single elements were reduced to their essential form to appear like symbols: the rocky embankment and the fortress, the trees, each single rippling wave, the archers and the garrison of the fortress. For such precise renderings of military undertakings

Curtius used the descriptive term "Annals written in pictures."

Even more obviously pictorial annals are seen in the bronze strips of the gates of Balawat from the reign of Ashurnasirpal's son Shalmaneser III (858–824 B.C.), from which Curtius chose to reproduce the representation of the king at the source of the Tigris [Fig. 70]. He pointed out that this Assyrian creation of continuous historical

Fig. 69. Relief from the throne-room of Ashurnasirpal II showing fugitives crossing the river at Carchemish, British Museum (after Henri Frankfort, *The Art and Architecture of the Ancient Orient.* 4th rev. ed., Baltimore: Penguin Books, 1970, Fig. 125).

narrative must have emerged from a specifically historical sense and that it is found again only on the columns of Trajan and Marcus Aurelius.

Curtius found that the most grandiose attempts at constructing a new pictorial unit belonged to the art of Kings Sennacherib (704–681 B.C.) and Ashurbanipal (668–627 B.C.). Curtius assumed that there was only one palace at Nineveh, now called the SW-palace of Sennach-

erib, which Ashurbanipal used before building his own
North-Palace.

The constraint of the single band of representation was
given up in Sennacherib's reliefs in favor of a general
mountainous background. Curtius was reminded of the
Naram-Sin stele as well as of medieval paintings which
show the sleeping apostles with Christ in the Garden all
occupying the same landscape. Curtius called this the

Fig. 70. Assyrians at the source of the Tigris. Detail from the bronze
bands of the gates at Balawat made for King Shalmaneser III, 883-824 B.C.,
British Museum (after Frankfort Art and Architecture, Fig. 91).

contracting manner of representation, which he also
claimed was an Assyrian discovery.

The best example is the scene of the transport of a bull
colossus. Above is a strip of the mountainous landscape
with botanically correctly rendered trees. Below, another
band shows the royal guardsmen. This, said Curtius, was
still the old manner of representation, but now a completely new image appears: a great scene is viewed from
a high vantage point [Fig. 71]. Deep down below is a

river, and—the beginning of true perspective—the water scoopers are rendered in half the size of the other figures on the sandbank between the river and the canal. As Curtius pointed out, ancient art never again came as close to the solution of perspective. Our image belongs to a large sequence, not entirely preserved, which shows the transport of a great, crudely blocked-out bull colossus,

Fig. 71. Moving a human-headed bull colossus. Detail of relief of Sennacherib, King of Assyria, 784-681 B.C., British Museum (after John Russell, *The Art Bulletin* LXIX, 1978, p. 526, Fig. 7).

coming from the quarry on a path both on land and in the water.

According to Curtius, the battle and hunting scenes were themes taken over from the archaic style. In the representations of technical procedures, however, the interest of the period in itself is evident. The Assyrian king enjoyed feelings of domination not only in military campaigns east and west, but also in organizing vast building activities. This image too has its dramatic tension, which is expressed in the movements of the engineers atop the colossus, and the effect is all the more visible because of the austere and factual rendering of the event.

Four years ago, knowledge of Sennacherib's inscriptions and a renewed visual analysis of these reliefs enabled John Russell, to write the article "Bulls for the Palace and Order in the Empire" *Art Bulletin* (1987), interpreting these works as an outcome of the king's concepts of the meaning of his rule. Yet it is interesting to observe how much valid information Curtius was able to gain from the mere examination of the reliefs themselves. He gave equally careful attention to the battle reliefs of Ashurbanipal and concluded that the reason art history ignores these works is because they are difficult of access and demand an effort to understand them. Therefore, these great images have not received the place in the history of world art which is due to them. Though written in 1923, his view still has validity.

When I first came to the Metropolitan Museum of Art in 1944, I found the fragments of Assyrian reliefs of Sennacherib and Ashurbanipal completely fascinating. They were only small pieces of the great panels that Curtius had discussed, but each one evoked an aspect of Assyrian life in which warfare played a major role. One of the reliefs shows cavalrymen leading their horses along a stream in a mountainous country [Fig. 72]. Another relief shows a soldier with his horse fording a river by appearing to walk upright through the waves and among the fish [Fig. 73]. Still another fragment shows a boat carrying captive women guarded by an Assyrian soldier [Fig. 74].

At that time, I mistakenly assigned this last fragment to Sennacherib. It was only a few years later when Margarethe Falkner of Graz took a few scholars through the gallery of the British Museum with the Sennacherib and Ashurbanipal reliefs, that I learned from her how to differentiate between them. She had recognized differ-

Fig. 72. Cavalrymen leading their horses, fragment of a relief of Sennacherib, Metropolitan Museum of Art.

ences in the military accoutrements, the most easily recognizable of which is the length of the armor shirt, which ends at the waist in the reliefs of Ashurbanipal. Of course, it was not only the small details but also the gestures, the composition, and, above all, the character of the scenes that made it possible to distinguish between the art of the two kings. For example, in the Ashurbanipal

Fig. 73. Cavalryman fording a river, fragment from a relief of Sennacherib, Metropolitan Museum of Art.

relief, a woman sitting in the boat, raising her hands before her face and leaning forward in a pose of utter dejection, is a more expressive figure than those seen in the marsh scenes of Sennacherib. Margarethe Falkner had noted such difference in the approach of Ashurbanipal's

Fig. 74. Assyrian soldiers guarding women captives in a boat, fragment from a relief of Ashurbanipal, King of Assyria, 668-627 B.C., Metropolitan Museum of Art.

sculptors and those of Sennacherib. An early death terminated her promising career.

In order to understand Assyrian art, one should wonder about the drive behind the extraordinary effort of the kings, particularly Sennacherib and Ashurbanipal, to have so much labor devoted to relief decoration.

I believe that the answer may be forthcoming not directly from the representation of military victories but from those showing monstrous or demonic figures [Fig. 5], for such reliefs are not as far apart from the military scenes as one might expect. In fact, our fragment with the captive women in a boat probably came from a room next to the one Barnett called the "Susiana room" in his volume on the reliefs in the North Palace of Ashurban-ipal. This room with a single entrance, contained reliefs depicting the assault and capture of the Elamite city of Hamanu and the exodus of prisoners from it on three walls as well as apotropaic figures in the large recess in the north-west wall. The doorjambs had identical pairs of apotropaic figures.

In a Babylonian text about such figures, which F. A. M. Wiggermann called Big-weather-beasts, a person who may have been a conjuration priest is ordered to draw two figures of Big-weather-beasts on the gate and to invest them with the power to defend the gate against aggressors (*Babylonian Prophylactic Figures*, p. 331). The same procedure and the effect may be assumed for the gate in this room of Ashurbanipal's palace. In addition, there was in the lower register under the Big-weather-beasts the relief showing a lion-man identified by Wiggermann as an *urmahlullu* [Fig. 75], a creature thought to protect lava-tories and bathrooms against Shulak, a lion or lioness-demon that haunted such rooms.

In view of the magic powers that the monstrous figures in the reliefs were assumed to control, one may wonder whether the reliefs showing military victories and rows of prisoners fulfilled merely a commemorative purpose.

More likely by eternalizing the effect of the enemies' defeat and misery they too were expected to influence future events.

Between the Neo-Assyrian empire and the Gudea-Ur III period (the early first millennium B.C. and the twentyfirst century B.C.), Mesopotamian art is largely represented by small cylinder seals. These are the objects that Christian had asked me to study and which continue to fascinate me today.

Those of the fourteenth to twelfth century B.C. in northern Mesopotamia represent the art of the Middle Assyrian period. To appreciate the design engraved on a slender stone cylinder it must be rolled over a flat surface of impressionable material like plasticene or some other product that can be hardened by baking. To illustrate how to appreciate a scene on a seal, I have chosen an ex-

Fig. 75. Human-headed lion, the *Urmah-lullu*. Drawing of a relief in the palace of Ashurbanipal (after Richard Barnett, *The Sculptures of the North Palace of Ashurbanipal at Nineveh, 668-627 B.C., London, 1976).*

ample [Fig. 76] that shows a lion menacing a fallen mountain sheep. The heavily muscled lion extends his body to touch the back of the sheep with one paw. He raises the other paw menacingly over his victim's head. A pine tree terminates the scene. A star fills what would otherwise be an empty space, but it may also be a meaningful symbol. Viewers of the small image should close their eyes and see if the memory of the image fills their entire inner vision. That is the way I see it. I assume other people working on seals have the same approach and I venture to suggest that the ancient seal cutter and probably the seal owner saw not a small but an enlarged design that expressed both the drama and the beauty of

Fig. 76. Lion attacking a mountain sheep. Modern impression of a cylinder seal, Middle Assyrian, ca. 13th century B.C., The Pierpont Morgan Library, No. 602.

the image. This is how seals should be viewed.

The meaning of scenes in which a lion or a hybrid monster attacks a horned game animal, which represent the majority of Middle Assyrian seal designs, is unknown. Perhaps they represent battles which were later pictured with human soldiers. The first person to draw attention to them and to the contemporary Kassite cylinders of Babylonia was Ernst Herzfeld, who had a very fine sense of style. The best work on cylinders of the period is the most recent, Donald Matthews, *Principles of Composition in Near Eastern Glyptic of the Late Second Millennium B.C.* (1990).

The seals of northern Mesopotamia and Syria in the fifteenth and early fourteenth centuries B.C., the time of the Mitannian empire, largely manifest a striking abstract

Fig. 77. Griffin and lion attacking a horned animal. Modern impression of a cylinder seal, Syro-Mitannian, ca. 15th-14th century B.C., The Pierpont Morgan Library, No. 1059.

style produced by mechanically rotated cutting wheels and drills [Fig. 77].

For the Old Babylonian art of the twentieth to the seventeenth century B.C. there is the stele of Hammurabi, which has long been known and analyzed, and there are clay plaques with various religious and ritual representations. Nevertheless, it is through the cylinder seals of the period that many of the deities and their emblems became known not only to the modern viewers but perhaps also to the ancients.

To interpret the meaning of the design on an Old Babylonian cylinder seal [Fig. 78] I cite just a statement by Wiggermann, "The representations of Old Babylonian seals reflect the religious interests of its bearer: defense against intruding evil, and good relations with

Fig. 78. King before the sun-god and other deities. Modern impression of a cylinder seal, Old Babylonian, ca. 1800 B.C., The Pierpont Morgan Library, No. 399.

the divine court, which ensures divine protection and well-being. These themes are the constituting elements of Mesopotamian prayers and incantations of all times . . ." (*Jaarbericht . . . ex oriente lux* 1987, p. 24). The scene shows the sun-god, as the chief justice of the world. He majestically places his foot on a hill holding the saw with which he "cuts decisions" as the chief justice of the world. This is a translation of the Akkadian term for judging. He majestically places his foot on a hill an act symbolic of ascending in the morning from the lap of heaven. This subject is repeated from the most delicate engravings at Sippar (his principal cult center) to the crudest carvings from the provinces. Commonly, the sun-god is approached by a king robed in a long mantle and offering a small goat. Cut on a smaller scale a diminutive priest with pail and sprinkler may represent the seal owner in a priestly function. A goddess with hands raised in supplication stands behind the king as a protective figure whose prayer may be directed for the benefit of the seal owner. The role of the male deity to the left of the group cannot be determined, while a goat placed beside another goddess, to the right, helps us identify the latter as a goddess, inspirer of correct interpretations of omens appearing in sacrifices. The uncertainties reflected above exemplify the difficulties which we still face today in interpreting ancient Near Eastern imagery, even if we are at a stage far more advanced than at the beginning of the century.

Major sculptures which first attracted the attention of the world's art lovers to the ancient Near East derive from the time of Gudea of Lagash, now known to have been an elder contemporary of Ur-Nammu, the first king of the Third Dynasty of Ur (2112–2094 B.C.). A recently published incense burner [Fig. 79] bears a dedication rendered here in a free translation: "For the well-being of Gudea, ruler of Lagash, and for her own well-being as well, Nin Alla, wife of Gudea, has dedicated this incense burner to Bawa, the gracious goddess, her mistress."

The small object, only 10.4 cm high, has a beautifully

Fig. 79. Censer dedicated by the wife of Gudea, Louvre
(after *La revue du Louvre* No. 1, 1991).

proportioned upper bowl. Its profile shows a smooth
molding bordered above by a thin one and below by two
more, one of which is slightly thicker and projects above

the lower one. The bowl rests on a gently spreading support. The combination of these abstract forms expresses the refined taste of the period, as exemplified in the sculptured bust of a noble lady [Fig. 80]. Curtius called the style classic because it reflected natural forms as in the soft folds of the garment over the arms yet retained the calm effect of the large surfaces. He noted the hands with the long fingers folded in a gesture of worship but expressing complete self-control, thereby creating an expression of aristocratic refinement and inner nervous life. Curtius added that nothing like this had been seen before the articulation of limbs in archaic Greek art. His remarks about these objects, now long known, are worthy of repetition because they retain the freshness and intensity of the impact of viewers as when they first appeared in photographs.

The powerfully muscular figure of Gudea [Fig. 65] presents an effective contrast to the refinement of the female sculpture [Fig. 80]. In a recent article Irene J. Winter harked back to verbal descriptions about Gudea's physical attributes, such as a strong arm, thus paralleling for the viewer visually and verbally the strength of Gudea as seen in his sculpture.

The foundation figure of King Ur-Nammu, 2112–2094 B.C. [Fig. 3a, b], shows the same muscular power in the figure of the king, even when emulating a lowly act, that of carrying a basket of earth or bricks for the building of a temple. His action was first portrayed in a third millennium B.C. relief from Tello, yet centuries later Ashurbanipal, the last great Assyrian king, is still seen raising the

Fig. 80. Fragmentary statue of a lady from the court of Gudea, Louvre (after *La revue du Louvre* No. 1, 1991).

basket "on his head like a holy crown" a phrase of Gudea's, in one of his building inscriptions.

To Henri Frankfort and Anton Moortgat, the two great art historians of the 1940s and 1950s Gudea's sculptures seemed less interesting than the Akkadian works because they lacked the immediacy and vitality of the preceding style of the dynasty of Akkad. According to Frankfort, "the technical achievements of the Akkadian period are utilized, but of the aspirations of that time not a trace remains. Piety replaces vigor." (*Art and Architecture*, p. 47). As for Moortgat: "In no statue of Gudea, however, has diorite . . . been moved and animated by the same inner restlessness and burning desire for action sometimes shown in the period of Manishtusu" (Moortgat, *The Art of Ancient Mesopotamia,* 1967, p. 62). There now appears a slight shift in the level of admiration for the classic style of Gudea and Ur-Nammu which we share with earlier art historians like Curtius.

The stele of Naram-Sin [Fig. 64] has amazed viewers since its discovery. Curtius described it particularly vividly, and I use his description here in a very free rendering of the German text because I think that he grasped not only what the artist represented but also the message intended for the viewer four thousand years ago, which probably does not differ greatly from that for the viewer of today. In an open landscape, a steep mountain is scaled by a group of soldiers on a narrow path. Gnarled trees characterize the rocky, wooded landscape. The king has sought to stage the decisive battle with the mountain peoples of the Lullubi on the summit, the pass where a tall rock rises. Now the decisive action has occurred. Two fallen enemies lie at the feet of Naram-Sin, almost in antithetic archaic postures. A third enemy has tumbled backward straight down the steep incline. The man trying to pull the deadly spear out of his neck is surely the enemy king. With his death, resistance ceases. The enemy begs for mercy. One of them has broken his spear as a sign of submission; another at the top, has thrown away his weapons and begs with raised hands, half in flight; a third, at a distance, waves, probably about to hide in the thicket and among the rocks.

*Arsis* (the rise) is created by soldiers ascending in identical stride, the lowest carrying the standards. *Akme* (the high point) is reached as the king stands alone, beside the mountain. Above are the constellations determining the event. The edge of the conical mountain forms the boundary between victor and vanquished. Here Naram-Sin places his foot on the corpses. The two main enemies are silhouetted against the conical plane of the mountain. In the descending composition, trees separate surrendering enemies from victorious soldiers. The king is the major figure. The ascending warriors look up to him; the defeated try to catch his eye. He is the first to have reached the top. Before him the power of the enemies has broken down.

As Curtius pointed out, all this is actually shown by modest means. The soldiers are represented by one type, and another type characterizes the vanquished enemies. Naram-Sin is rendered like one of the soldiers but he surpasses his enemies in size. However, he is only taller by just one head as he may have been described at the time. The scene, therefore, retains the human scale which makes the rendering of the event believable. Some of the effect is due to the modeling of the royal figure in high relief so that it stands out from the low background, giving it dramatic motion.

The genetic predecessors of the stele are still unknown as they were in the time of Curtius. Akkad, the capital of the dynasty since Sargon founded it, remains to be discovered. Its palace may have contained wall paintings with compositions that extended beyond the horizontal

Fig. 81. The flight of Etana to heaven. Modern impression of a cylinder seal, Akkadian, ca. 2340-2150 B.C., The Pierpont Morgan Library, No. 236.

bands that generally confined Mesopotamian compositions from monumental reliefs to small cylinder seals. However, a few cylinders of the Akkad period [Figs. 81-83], seem to transcend the horizontal rectangle that usually limited the design of a scene. For example, Etana, the shepherd king, is shown flying toward heaven with the help of an eagle [Fig. 81]. Dogs, seated on the ground, raise their heads to watch and shepherds lift their hands in wonderment at the sight. The composition is thus unified in its upward extension.

In a cylinder seal of the same period the upward extension of the picture plane in a hunting scene in the mountains is achieved by the outline of a mountain [Fig. 82]. Finally, in the seal of Adda in the British Museum [Fig. 83] the mountain pattern creates a common base for a group of gods. It also helps join Ishtar, whose abode is chiefly in heaven with the sun-god Shamash, who rises from beneath the horizons where he invisibly spends the

Fig. 82. Hunt in the mountains. Modern impression of a cylinder seal, Akkadian, ca. 2200 B.C., Museum of Fine Arts, Boston (after Edward Terrace, *The Art of the Ancient Near East in Boston*, 1962, Fig. 6).

night.

The above examples tend to show that the upward extension of a composition was used by seal engravers. While Curtius considered seal engraving as an independent, minor art, Frankfort thought that in Mesopotamia, "From Early Dynastic times decorative art in all its branches utilized the inventions of the seal cutters" (*Cylinder Seals*, p. 308). I agree with him to the extent that

I do not believe that there was a clear division within the craftsmanship of the Mesopotamian sculptors. That ivory workers could, on occasion, also work on major stone sculpture is demonstrable from India. An inscription on the south gateway of the Sanchi Stupa states that the work was done by the ivory carvers of Vedisa, the nearby capital. The sculpture on the gateway was certainly larger than the usual scale of ivory working and there was, of

Fig. 83. The rising sun-god and other deities. Modern impression of the cylinder seal of Adda, Akkadian, ca. 2300-2200 B.C., British Museum.

course, considerable difference in the technique. Yet, my colleague Vidya Dehejia informs me that in India the same craftsmen worked in stone and bronze until about the ninth century A.D.

Ludwig Curtius began his study of Mesopotamian art with an analysis of cylinder seals of the Early Dynastic period whose insights and thoroughness were unmatched until the work of Frankfort and Moortgat. Curtius's study was centered on seal impressions deriving from the court of the Sumerian ruler Lugalanda of Lagash [Fig. 84]. In the course of his analysis he discovered some of the essential characteristics of the style that we now call Early Dynastic III B.

Fig. 84. Drawings of ancient impressions of cylinder seals of Lugalanda of Lagash, ca. 2360 B.C. (after Henri Frankfort, *Cylinder Seals*, London, 1939, p. 53, figs. 20, 21).

The seals he studied show a frieze of struggling heroes, animals, and predators contained within the rectangular area of the mantle of a cylinder. The figures tightly fill the space with vertical axes dividing the overlapping figures. All heads are kept at the same height as if conforming to a law, the term for which is isokephaly. There is a balanced relationship between the postures of the figures, which have a geometric character. The figures are not merely aligned in continuous friezes but also appear as compositional elements in heraldic motifs, best seen on the silver vase of Entemena, ca. 2450 B.C. [Fig. 34] These images show a subjugation of the natural figure to formal concepts of rhythm and of a limiting space. They belong to a decorative style which Curtius recognized as the first of its kind in the history of art. He pointed out that the lion-headed eagle, which dominates the design in the Entemena vase, derives its timeless abstract character from its frontal stylization. The animals that the eagle grasps are as directionless as the principal figure because their movements balance each other. But the single animals are deprived of their uniqueness by the repetition of the motif, and in the end they are transformed into a continuous frieze by the lions biting the horned animals. Curtius characterized this art as lacking every expression of the naive, cheerful life which Egyptian art loved so dearly. In fact, he aptly described the art of Western Asia as "humorless." Without having any factual evidence for a long development of art before the Entemena vase, he assumed that generations must have worked to develop the laws according to which the designs of the vase were composed. Indeed, almost a thousand years separate the beginnings of Mesopotamian art in the Uruk period from the Entemena vase.

For the origin of Mesopotamian cylinder seals, of monumental architecture and sculpture, we have to go to to about 3300 B.C. to the site of Uruk/Warka in southern

Mesopotamia. There we also find the origins of a coherent narration in the Warka vase, later found again in the Naram-Sin stele.

The great alabaster vase [Fig. 85] was discovered at Uruk/Warka in the winter of 1933/34 and published by Ernst Heinrich, whose text is used as a basis for the following description. The vase was part of a large collection of objects we call the *Sammelfund.* There were animals sculptured in the round; cylinder seals, stamp seals, and seal impressions on lumps of clay; vessels of stone, plain and ornamented, pottery and metal vessels; beads and pieces of jewellery; ornaments of structures, furniture and tools; and various other items. The interpretation now favored of the circumstances leading to the *Sammelfund* is that an enemy plundered a storage

Fig. 85. Alabaster vase from Uruk, last quarter of the fourth millennium B.C. (after Strommenger *5000 Years,* Pl. 19).

place of movable temple inventory which could have been a treasury.

The vase was produced from a large piece of alabaster by slow manual labor with stone instruments and abrasives. It is shaped like a chalice with a conical foot with slightly everted rim. The height of the body with the reliefs measures about 92 cm. The representations are applied to three circular registers measuring 25 cm., 17.5 cm. and 20 cm. in width, the lowest is bisected horizontally [Fig. 86].

The contents of the reliefs of the three registers obviously belong together; they apparently relate a gift to the Eanna sanctuary. The action begins in the top register.

The presence of the goddess Inanna is indicated by her symbol, the ring bundle, two examples of which occupy the entire height of the top register. Behind the symbols, offerings of all types are set up and laid down. These include two large vessels with the fruits of field and garden; two tall, footed chalices in shape similar to the great vase; two low, footed bowls, which surely contained some fine substance; two vessels in the form of small animal figurines, representing a gazelle and a lion; two square objects which cannot be interpreted; a bull's head; and an object which looks like a quiver with an attached lid. Most important is a curious group of figures: two maned rams placed closely together carry on their backs a two-stepped pedestal to which ring bundles are attached. These associate the whole group with the goddess Inanna. On each step stands the figure of a man. One of them has his hands raised, grasping with one hand the wrist of the other, the other man holds with outstretched hands an object, the form of which occurs in the older

Fig. 86. Drawing of scenes on the alabaster vase from Uruk (after André Parrot, *Sumer*, Paris, 1960, Fig. 89).

levels of Layer III and, according to Falkenstein is to be read EN—lord.

In front of the large ring bundles stands a figure that appears to be characterized as female by her garment. It does not hang from the belt, as in the figures of men, but it covers the upper body and the left arm. Only the right arm remains free. The garment seems to consist of a textile which is edged but not sewn in any other way. The woman's profile is differentiated only very slightly from that of the other figures: mouth and chin recede a little. Her hair falls in a wider bunch on the back than that of the men. She wears a headgear which leaves a narrow strip of hair free on the forehead. In the back of her head there is a horn-shaped point and there was surely a similar one in front which was lost in antiquity with a piece of the rim of the vessel. The woman has her right hand raised, much as the deities in later cylinders in the presentation scenes. This gesture as well as her position before the two Inanna symbols and her direction toward the people bringing the offerings mark the woman as the person who accepts the donations, regardless of whether one interprets her as the goddess herself or only as her reprensentative, her priestess.

The first figure of the procession, that moves toward the woman is a nude man who carries a vessel filled with fruit, very similar to those already set up behind the ring bundles. The following figure is obviously the principal one, the leader of the procession. Unfortunately all that is preserved of that figure are one foot, a part of the garment, and the long plaited or woven belt with two large tassels at the end, which is carried by a servant behind him. The garment has a broad seam and is patterned by closely placed crossed lines.

The second register continues the row of offerers which begins above with the first figure of the procession. The third register shows the herds dedicated to the goddess, her gardens and fields. The wavy line below indicates the river. Above it is a row of the plants which grow from it. They were originally identified as ears of grain and date palms, but the latter have now been recognized as flax which indicates a connection with an early textile industry.

This vase is the first extant monument which presents

pictorially an orderly, continuous account of an event. In short, it is history's first narrative representation.

The relief of the vase is not the earliest at Uruk because fragments of artificial stone with considerable use of gypsum were found at Uruk by Lenzen and discussed again by Eva Strommenger. These reliefs of artifical stone must have been cast. For them to be cast, there must have been a mold. Whatever technique was used for the mold, it was negative in relation to the figure which was to be

Fig. 87. Priestly ruler bringing offerings. Modern impression of a cylinder seal, Uruk, ca. 3000 B.C. (after Anton Moortgat, *The Art of Ancient Mesopotamia*, London, 1969, Pl. A,6).

produced. In other words, the artist went through the same creative process as did the seal cutter when carving a design. In his imagination he is inside the object that he models, working against its skin.

Now to a cylinder seal design of the ruler figure [Fig. 87] in what is referred to as the *Netzrock*, a netted skirt, identified as a diaphanous garment, because the legs are visible through it. I explain this representation in the following way: I believe that the ruler figure was designed as a whole. The Uruk artist saw the male body as an organic unit. He carved it as that and then dressed it in a skirt of patterned material, which he indicated by criss-crossing. The impressions of such seals seem to me to show that the dress was added secondarily. In my opinion, this has created the impression of a diaphanous material.

Turning to the representation of the ruler on the vase, I suggest that the fact that the leg is outlined under the garment, probably indicates that the technique in which it was carved derived both from the earlier, artificial stone, which was cast, and from carved cylinder seals. In both the body could have been modeled first, the garment carved over it later.

The concern with the attire of the figure indicates its importance. It represents the dominant male personage of the period, the figure of a ruler. It is not surprising, therefore, that a three-dimensional sculpture of such a figure [Fig. 88] turned up in the excavations of Uruk several years after the vase.

Surely, the latter part of the fourth millennium B.C. was the time of the self-realization of Mesopotamian man, symbolized by the figure of the ruler. There must have been a recognition of his potential and his responsibility for leadership, as a builder of lasting structures and as a being with the power to change and direct the life that nature had provided for him and his people.

Earlier, in 1939, a life-size female head was found at Warka [Fig 89]. The eyebrows and eyes which were inlaid in a different material, have disappeared. Nevertheless, the effect of the head is extraordinarily vivid. Lenzen, the

Fig. 88. Male statuette from Uruk, third quarter of the fourth millennium B.C. (after Strommenger *5000 Years*, Pl. 33).

excavator, ascribed this to the natural carving of the eyelids. The eyebrows repeat in beautifully curving lines the almond shape of the eyes. The cheekbones are broad and stressed but not exaggerated. The mouth is tightly closed, the chin is strong and softened by a slightly indicated double chin. Henri Frankfort noted that the artist's main interest seemed to have been the living flesh. In my opinion, the artist's aim was the rendering of the human being, as in the male torso. Even if the purpose was the rendering of a goddess, as is generally assumed, she was conceived in the image of a human woman as the artist who sculpted the work was fully aware.

It is interesting to contrast my remarks with Frankfort's view of the style of the "proto-literate" period as represented in the sculptures and cylinders of Uruk in relation to the abstract style manifested in Early Dynastic sculptures from Tell Asmar in northern Mesopotamia [Fig. 90]. Having originally considered the style of Tell Asmar the

Fig. 89. Female head from Uruk, third quarter of the fourth millennium B.C. (after Strommenger *5000 Years* Pl. 31).

Fig. 90. Group of statues from the Abu Temple at Tell Asmar, Diyala region, ca. 2800-2600 B.C. (after Frankfort *Art and Architecture*, Pl. 13).

first manifestation of Mesopotamian sculpture, Frankfort had to come to terms with the then newly found earlier and strikingly naturalistic works. He expressed the opinion that the Uruk style had been ousted (by the artists of Tell Asmar) when they came to believe that "the translation of the ever changing world of appearance into the stable form of sculpture could be achieved only by a bold grasp of essential shapes shorn of accidentals to such an extent that they approach geometrical forms."—This view may be understood only as the result of the intellectual attitude that saw in the style of cubism an ultimate truth rather than a passing style of Western European art. But as has been shown in this essay (though this is expressly stated only in this last instance), such "passing styles" influence the views of their contemporaries and the understanding of ancient art to which every generation makes its own contribution. Today we consider the Tell Asmar sculptures a provincial manifestation even though its creators produced some masterpieces. How they will be assessed by future art historians cannot be foretold.

[The photographs in this section were contributed by David A. Loggie, Chief Photographer, The Pierpont Morgan Library, in memory of Dr. Edith Porada.]

# NOTES

## MAN AND IMAGES IN THE ANCIENT NEAR EAST

[1]W. Lambert, "The Relationship of Sumerian and Babylonian Myth as Seen in Accounts of Creation," *La circulation des biens, des personnes et des idées dans le Proche-Orient ancien: Actes de la XXXVIIIe rencontre assyriologique internationale* (Paris: Editions Recherche sur les Civilisations, 1992), pp. 129–193.

[2]See Jeremy Black and Anthony Green, *Gods, Demons, and Symbols of Ancient Mesopotamia: An Illustrated Dictionary* (London: The British Museum Press, 1992), p. 75.

[3]For a discussion of this cylinder see my article, "Notes on the Sargonid Cylinder Seal, Ur 364," *Iraq* 22 (1960), pp. 116–123.

[4]The cylinder is No. 202 in the catalogue of the collection of the Pierpont Morgan Library that was published by me in *Corpus of Ancient Near Eastern Seals in North American Collections, Vol. 1, The Collection of the Pierpont*

*Morgan Library* (Washington: Bollingen Foundation, 1948), cited in this essay as *Morgan*.

[5] Apsu is the freshwater ocean, see Black and Green, p. 27, s.v. *abzu*.

[6] For comments on the figurine and good photographs see Betty L. Schlossman, "Two Foundation Figurines," in *Ancient Mesopotamian Art and Selected Texts: The Pierpont Morgan Library* (New York: Pierpont Morgan Library, 1976), pp. 9–21.

[7] Dominique Beyer, C. Forrières, F. Bargain, F. Lemaire, "Les lions du temple du «roi du pays» de Mari," *Mari 7* (Paris: Editions Recherche sur les Civilisations, 1993), pp. 79–105.

[8] See Erica Reiner's reference to text No. 253 in "Another Volume of Sultantepe Tablets," *Journal of Near Eastern Studies* 26 (1967), p. 192, where she cites the drawing of protective demons. Wiggermann cites this reference in his book, *Mesopotamian Protective Spirits: The Ritual Texts* (Groningen: Styx & PP Publications, 1992), pp. 35-36 and notes 4 and 7, where he refers to the preparation of a paste with "*šadânu ṣābitu*-stone" to be used for the drawing of a figure of "the lord" and two figures of "big weather beasts . . ." These are leonine monsters which I call lion-demons, or lion-griffins.

[9] Henry N. Michael and Ye. D. Prokofyeva, "The Costume of an Enets Shaman," in *Studies in Siberian Shamanism,* Anthropology of the North: Translations from Russian Sources, no. 4 (Toronto: Published for the Arctic Institute of North America by University of Toronto Press, 1963), pp. 124–156.

[10] See Michael and Prokofyeva, p. 124.

[11]Pasztory, E., "Shamanism and North American Indian Art," in *Native North American Art History,* Z. P. Mathews and A. Jonaitis, eds. (Palo Alto, Ca.: Peek Publications, 1982) pp. 7–30.

[12]Pasztory, *Shamanism.*

[13]See Pasztory, *Shamanism,* p. 9.

[14]For the original publication of this frequently reproduced design see L. Capitan, H. Breuil, I. Bourmet, P. Peyrony, "Abri Mêge, une station magadalénienne," *Revue de l'École d'Anthropologie de Paris* XIV (1906), pp. 198–212.

[15]R. L. Solecki and T. McGovern, "Predatory Birds and Prehistoric Man," in *Theory and Practice: Essays Presented to Gene Weltfish,* S. Diamond, ed. (New York: Mouton Publishers, 1980), pp. 79–95.

[16]R. L. Solecki, "Predatory Bird Rituals at Zawi Chemi Shanidar," *Sumer* XXXIII (1977) p. 45. For the painting from Çatal Hüyük, see James Mellaart, *Çatal Hüyük, a Neolithic Town in Anatolia* (London: Thames and Hudson, 1967), fig. 47, p. 169.

[17]The figure belongs to Robin B. Martin and is on loan at the Brooklyn Museum; the photographs are published here with his permission.

[18]E. Porada, "Seals and Related Objects from Early Mesopotamia and Iran," in *Early Mesopotamia and Iran: Contact and Conflict, 3500–1600 B.C.,* John Curtis, ed. (London: The British Museum Press, 1993), pp. 44–53.

[19]Michael and Prokofyeva, p. 129.

[20]See the article by Randall White, "The Earliest Images: Ice Age 'Art' in Europe," *Expedition* 34, no. 3 (1992) pp. 37–51.

²¹See S.K. Kozlowski, ed., *Nemrik 9, Pre-Pottery Neolithic Site in Iraq: General Report, Seasons 1985–1986* (Warszawa: Wydawnictwa Uniwersytetu Warszawskiego, 1990); also "Nemrik 9, A PPN Neolithic Site in Northern Iraq," *Paléorient* 15/1, 1989 (1990), pp. 25–31. Also Trevor Watkins, "Pushing Back the Frontiers of Mesopotamian Prehistory," *The Biblical Archaeologist*, vol. 55, no. 4 (Dec. 1992), pp. 176–181.

²²In a personal letter Professor Kozlowski also mentioned a female figurine, a man's phallic sculpture, a leopard, a snake, the foot of a bovine animal, birds in different stages of completion, and a vulture in an extremely interesting position. We hope to hear Professor Kozlowski and see his slides in a meeting of the Columbia Seminar on Feb. 9, 1995.

²³R. de Mecquenem, L. LeBreton, M. Rutten, *Archéologie susienne*, Mémoires de la mission archéologique en Iran XXX (Paris: Presses Universitaires de France, 1947), fig. 51, no. 19.

²⁴I owe this negative result to my assistant, Allison Karmel, whom I asked to make a survey of the published material.

²⁵Arthur J. Tobler, *Excavations at Tepe Gawra II* (Philadelphia: Published for the University Museum by University of Pennsylvania Press, 1950), pl. CLXIII, p. 81.

²⁶Henri Frankfort, *Oriental Institute Discoveries in Iraq, 1933/34*, The Oriental Institute of the University of Chicago, Oriental Institute Communications, no. 19 (Chicago: University of Chicago Press, 1935), p. 29, fig. 30.

²⁷For the stamp seals of the Chalcolithic period in Iran see my article "Cylinder Seals," in *Encyclopaedia Iranica*

VI: 5 (1993), pp. 479–505. The words "Iran and Iranian" have been changed by the editor to "Persia and Persian" without obtaining my consent.

[28]The male figures on stamp seals from Değirmentepe in the Malatya region of Turkey, however, differ in not having a goat. "The Chalcolithic Occupation at Değirmentepe (Malatya) in Eastern Turkey," in *Studi di Paletnologia in onore di Salvatore M. Puglisi,* M. Liverani, A. Palmieri, R. Peroni, eds. (Rome: Università di Roma "La Sapienza," 1985), pp. 253–263.

[29]For the details concerning the figure see Edith Porada, "A Man with Serpents," in *Von Uruk nach Tuttul, eine Festschrift für Eva Strommenger: Studien und Aufsätze von Kollegen und Freunden,* B. Hrouda, S. Kroll and P. Z. Spanos, eds., Münchener vorderasiatische Studien, Bd. 12 (München: Profil, 1992), pp. 171–175.

[30]"A foreign captive. From a royal mortuary temple of the Sixth Dynasty at Saḳḳāreh," William C. Hayes, *The Scepter of Egypt I,* 5th printing, rev. (New York: Metropolitan Museum of Art, 1990), fig. 67, p. 114.

[31]See Porada, "Man with Serpents," pl. 74.

[32]Observation made by Jonathan Rosen in a seminar held at the Pierpont Morgan Library in the autumn semester of 1993.

[33]See my note 32.

[34]Oral observation on the basis of the drawings fig. 26 a,b by Ursula Seidl Calmeyer, August 1993.

[35]F. A. M. Wiggermann, "Exit Talim! Studies in Babylonian Demonology, Part I," *Jaarbericht van het Vooraziatisch-Egyptisch Genootschap Ex Oriente Lux,* no. 27 (1981-82), pp. 90–105.

[36]W. B. Emery, *Archaic Egypt* (Baltimore: Penguin Books, 1967), pl. 3(a).

[37]F. A. M. Wiggermann, *Mesopotamian Protective Spirits*, pp. 148 ff.

[38]As far as I know, he has not given the reasons for the identification of the ibex with Enki, though this is entirely possible.

[39]Stags were identified with Ninhursag because of their occurrence on the temple of the goddess at Ubaid. H. R. Hall and C. L. Woolley, *Ur Excavations. I: Al-ʿUbaid* (London: The British Museum, 1934), pl. VI.

[40]Wiggermann, *Mesopotamian Protective Spirits*, p. 160.

[41]The most important article on Late Early Dynastic cylinder seals is that of D. P. Hansen, "The Fantastic World of Sumerian Art: Seal Impressions from Ancient Lagash," in *Monsters and Demons in the Ancient and Medieval Worlds: Papers Presented in Honor of Edith Porada,* A. E. Farkas, P. O. Harper, and E. B. Harrison, eds. (Mainz: Philipp von Zabern, 1987), pp. 53–63.

[42]Gudrun Selz, *Die Bankettszene: Entwicklung eines 'Überzeitlichen' Bildmotivs in Mesopotamien von der frühdynastischen bis zur Akkad-zeit,* Freiburger alt orientalische Studien, Bd. 11 (Wiesbaden: F. Steiner, 1983); also Julia M. Asher-Greve, *Frauen in altsumerischer Zeit*, Bibliotheca Mesopotamica, v. 18 (Malibu: Undena, 1985), pp. 97 ff.

[43]See P. R. S. Moorey, "What Do We Know about the People Buried in the Royal Cemetery?" *Expedition* 20, no. 1 (1977), pp. 24–40.

[44]Rainer M. Boehmer, "Das Auftreten des Wasserbüffels in Mesopotamien in historischer Zeit und seine sum-

erische Bezeichnung," *Zeitschrift für Assyriologie und vorderasiatische Archäologie* 64 (1975), pp. 1–19.

[45]For the horned crown of Mesopotamian gods see Rainer M. Boehmer, "Die Entwicklung der Hörnerkrone von ihren Anfängen bis zum Ende der Akkad-Zeit," *Berliner Jahrbuch für Vor-und Frühgeschichte* 7 (1967), pp. 273–291.

[46]For this and all other themes of the Akkad period, see Rainer M. Boehmer, *Die Entwicklung der Glyptik während der Akkad-Zeit*, Untersuchungen zur Assyriologie und vorderasiatischen Archäologie, Bd. 4 (Berlin: W. de Gruyter, 1965).

[47]David and Joan Oates, "Excavations at Tell Brak, 1990-91," *Iraq* 53 (1991), p. 136, fig. 4 and pl. 28c.

[48]Wiggermann, *Mesopotamian Protective Spirits*, p. 169, s.v. *ugallu*="Big Weather Beast."

[49]For a general outline of the sequence of cylinder seal styles see my article, "Why Cylinder Seals?: Engraved Cylindrical Seal Stones of the Ancient Near East, Fourth to First Millennium B.C.," *The Art Bulletin* LXXV, no. 4 (1993), pp. 563–582.

[50]For Old Babylonian terracotta reliefs see Ruth Opificius, *Das altbabylonische Terrakottarelief*, Untersuchungen zur Assyriologie und vorderasiatische Archäologie, Bd. 2, (Berlin: W. de Gruyter, 1961); Marie-Thérèse Barrelet, *Figurines et reliefs en terre cuite de la Mésopotamie antique*, L'Institut français d'archéologie de Beyrouth, Bibliothèque archéologique et historique, t. 85 (Paris: Librairie orientaliste Paul Geuthner, 1968); P. R. S. Moorey, "The Terracotta Plaques from Kish and Hursagkalama, c. 1850 to 1650 B.C.," *Iraq* 37 (1975), pp. 79–99;

NOTES

Evelyn Klengel-Brandt, *Die Terrakotten aus Assur im Vorderasiatischen Museum, Berlin* (Berlin: Deutscher Verlag der Wissenschaften, 1978).

[51]For examples of the bull-man and the nude bearded hero with curls on clay plaques see the works cited in my note 50.

[52]For "Humbaba" (Sumerian: Huwawa) see Black and Green, p. 106.

[53]Wiggermann, *Mesopotamian Protective Spirits*, excerpts from pp. 6 ff.

[54]Martine van Loon wrote to me that she found that cornel wood was equivalent to our dogwood.

[55]See the description by C. L. Woolley, *Ur Excavations II: The Royal Cemetery* (London: The British Museum, 1934), p. 81: ". . . immediately behind the bowl, (37) was a group of gold chisels, U. 10429-33, and a gold saw, U. 10428; with them and probably belonging to their handles were three rings of gold binding, U. 10443; just beside them, against the woodwork of the chariot, were two bronze axes, U. 10416 and U. 10418, a whetstone, U. 10419, and all together and right against the chisels a cluster of nineteen wooden balls (U. 10434) which are perhaps gaming-counters. Between the stone bowl and the chest were . . . two bronze axes with gold binding of type A 12, U. 10435, and at (34) a gaming board, U. 10478."

[56]Stefan M. Maul, "Auf meinen Rechtsfall werde doch aufmerksam. Wie sich die Babylonier und Assyrer vor Unheil schützten, das sich durch ein Vorzeichen angekündigt hatte," *Mitteilungen der Deutschen Orient-Gesellschaft zu Berlin* 124 (1992), pp. 131–142.

[57]For a survey article on Lamashtu see Walter Farber, "Lamaštu," in *Reallexikon der Assyriologie und vorderasiatischen Archäologie*, Bd. 6 (Berlin: W. de Gruyter, 1983), pp. 439–446; also "Tamarisken-Fibeln-Skolopender: zur philologischen Deutung der 'Reiseszene' auf neuassyrischen Lamaštu-Amuletten," in *Language, Literature, and History: Philological and Historical Studies Presented to Erica Reiner*, F. Rochberg-Halton, ed., American Oriental Series, vol. 67 (New Haven, Conn.: American Oriental Society, 1987), pp. 85–105.

[58]F. A. M. Wiggermann, "Lamaštu, Dochter van Anu," in M. Stol, *Zwangerschap en geboorte bij de Babyloniërs en in de Bijbel*, pp. 95–116.

[59]P. R. S. Moorey, "A Bronze 'Pazuzu' Statuette from Egypt," *Iraq* XXVII (1965), pp. 33–41.

[60]Cited by Maul, p. 131.

[61]The Hebrew actually only has the word "idols" as Allison Karmel informs me.

[62]There were degrees of reality; see T. Jacobsen, "The Graven Image," in *Ancient Israelite Religion: Essays in Honor of Frank Moore Cross*, P. D. Miller, P. D. Hanson, and S. D. McBride, eds. (Philadelphia: Fortress Press, 1987), pp. 15–37.

## DISCUSSION

[1]D. Opitz, *Archiv für Orientforschung* 6 (1930-1931), pp. 61-62, Tf. III, Fig. 2; H. Frankfort, *Cylinder Seals: A Documentary Essay on the Art and Religion of the Ancient Near East*, London (1939) 131 and pl. XXIIk; R. M. Boehmer, *Die Entwicklung der Glyptik während der Akkad-Zeit*, Berlin (1965), p. 118 and Abb. 353.

[2]W. G. Lambert and A. R. Millard, *Atra-Ḫasīs: The Babylonian Story of the Flood*, Oxford (1969).
[3]The cosmogony of the third millennium B.C. is treated by F. A. M. Wiggermann, "Mythological Foundations of Nature," in *Natural Phenomena: Their Meaning, Depiction and Description in the Ancient Near East*, D. J. W. Meijer, ed., Amsterdam (1992), pp. 279-300.
[4]Further examples concern the killing of the monster Humbaba by Gilgamesh and Enkidu (on clay plaques and seals from the early second millennium B.C. onwards) and Etana's flight to heaven on the back of an eagle (on Akkadian seals), corresponding respectively to scenes from the *Epic of Gilgamesh* (see note 6) and the *Legend of Etana*, for which see J. V. Kinnier Wilson, *The Legend of Etana: A New Edition*, Warminster (1985).
[5]Photograph and brief commentary in W. Orthmann, *Der alte Orient*, Propyläen Kunstgeschichte XIV, Berlin (1975) pl. IX and pp. 192f.; see also S. A. Rashid, *Mesopotamien Musikgeschichte in Bildern*, Bd. 2, Lfg. 2, Leipzig (1984), p. 40 and Abb. 8. For further literature and a treatment see F. A. M. Wiggermann, "Scenes from the Shadow Side," in *Metaphorical Language in Ancient Mesopotamian Literature*, H. L. J. Vanstiphout and M. E. Vogelzang, eds., Groningen (1994, in press).
[6]M. Gallery Kovacs, *The Epic of Gilgamesh*, Stanford (1989), p. 76 (Tablet IX).
[7]Winged beings and fabulous animals are treated in F. A. M. Wiggermann, "Mischwesen," in *Reallexikon der Assyriologie*, Berlin (1994, in press).
[8]"Big City" is one of the names of the Other World (Netherworld), see Wiggermann, "Shadow Side."

# NOTES

[9]W. Stauder, "Asinus ad Lyram," in *Frankfurter Kunsthistorische Studien: Festschrift Helmuth Ostoff*, Tutzing (1969), pp. 25-32.

[10]Edited by F. Köcher, "Der Babylonische Göttertypentext," *Mitteilungen des Instituts für Orientforschung* 1 (1953), pp. 57-107.

[11]These texts cannot be treated here in detail. Some citations can be found in Wiggermann, "Shadow Side."

[12]Cf. J. Bottéro and S. N. Kramer, "Victoire d'Inanna sur l'Ebih" (translation and commentary), in *Lorsque les dieux faisaient l'homme*, Paris (1989), pp. 219.

[13]For rays emanating from the mountain see Boehmer, *Entwicklung der Glyptik*, Abb. 300.

[14]Cf. E. Cassin, *La splendeur divine*, Paris (1968); A. L. Oppenheim, *Ancient Mesopotamia: Portrait of a Dead Civilization*, rev. ed. completed by Erica Reiner, Chicago (1977), p. 98 ("awe-inspiring luminosity").

[15]The scorpion-man, too, sometimes has rays coming from his body, see E. Porada, ed., *Ancient Art in Seals*, Princeton (1980) Fig. II-20.

[16]The part of the enemy can be played by mountain gods, monsters, or wild animals (sometimes supplied with wings); see the discussion in Wiggermann, "Mischwesen."

[17]Those animal spirits that developed into monsters (composite creatures) were treated by F. A. M. Wiggermann, *Mesopotamian Protective Spirits: The Ritual Texts*, Groningen (1992), pp. 147ff.

[18]Cf. Wiggermann, *Mesopotamian Protective Spirits*, pp. 180f.

[19]Cf. W. G. Lambert, "Išḫara," in *Reallexikon der Assyri-*

*ologie*; J. S. Cooper, "Heilige Hochzeit," in *Reallexikon der Assyriologie*, § 16.

[20]The Early Dynastic iconographical theme of a boat-god sailing through a cosmic ocean in the company of a number of seemingly unrelated objects (plough, vessel, lion, cosmic scorpion) may have a calendrical meaning, see Wiggermann, "Mischwesen."

[21]For this goddess see the literature cited in note 19. The meaning (and the linguistic affiliation) of her name has not yet been established; there is a good possibility, however, that her name simply means "Scorpion", and is related to our "scorpion" (root *shar/skar*).

[22]H. G. Gundel, *Zodiakos: Tierkreisbilder im Altertum*, Mainz (1992), pp. 20, 29. See also H. G. Gundel, *Zodiakos: Der Tierkreis in der antiken Literatur und Kunst. Mit einem Beitrag über den Tierkreis im Alten Orient von Robert Böker*, München (1972), and J. Koch, *Neue Untersuchungen zur Topographie des babylonischen Fixsternhimmels*, Wiesbaden (1989).

[23]A. W. Mair and G. R. Mair, trans., *Callimachus and Lycophoron; Aratus*, Loeb Classical Library, London (1921).

[24]See the literature cited in note 22.

[25]Recent studies of this figure are E. von der Osten-Sacken, *Der Ziegen-'Dämon'*, Neukirchener-Vluyn (1992); P. Amiet, "Le problème de l'iconographie divine en Mésopotamie dans la glyptique antérieure à l'époque d'Agade," in *Contributi e materiali di archeologia orientale* 1 (1986); and M. Matoušová, "Die tanzende Gottheit," *Archiv Orientální* 60 (1992), pp. 347-353.

[26]Von der Osten-Sacken, *Der Ziegen-'Dämon'*, 99ff.

# NOTES

[27]P. Amiet, *L'âge des échanges inter-iraniens,* Paris (1986), Ch. I; S. Pollock, "Power Politics in the Susa A Period," in *Upon This Foundation: The 'Ubaid Reconsidered,* E. F. Henrickson and I. Thuesen, eds., Copenhagen (1989), pp. 281ff.

[28]The seal on which the skirt is completely visible is von der Osten-Sacken, *Der Ziegen-'Dämon',* no. 48. On this seal the upturned points of the shoes are visible as well.

[29]See Å. W. Sjöberg and E. Bergmann, *The Collection of the Sumerian Temple Hymns,* Locust Valley, N.Y. (1969), p. 66[25].

[30]Von der Osten-Sacken, *Der Ziegen-'Dämon',* Fig. 51. The figure wears the same skirt as the ibex-god, but lacks the shoes with upturned points.

[31]Historical Mesopotamian culture does not seem to have preserved any traces of a prehistoric shamanism.

[32]On this god see Th. Jacobsen, "Description of Major Finds from Ishchali," in *Old Babylonian Public Buildings in the Diyala Region,* H. D. Hill, Th. Jacobsen, P. Delougaz, eds., Chicago (1990), pp. 99ff.; P. Michalowski, "Presence at the Creation," in *Lingering over Words: Studies in Ancient Near Eastern Literature in Honor of William L. Moran,* T. Abush et al. eds., Harvard (1990), pp. 381-396; A. Heidel, "The Meaning of 'Mummu' in Akkadian Literature," *Journal of Near Eastern Studies* 7 (1948), pp. 98-105; J. Bottéro, *Mythes et rites de Babylone,* Paris (1985), p. 117[4].

[33]There are some exceptional occurrences of a similar creature, for instance on the back of a Chimaera, cf. K. Schefold, *Frühgriechische Sagenbilder,* München (1964), Fig. 40b (ca. 610 B.C.).

[34]Mummu is the vizier (*sukkallu*) of Apsû. The vizier of a god often is his visible or audible manifestation. In the case of Mummu it is clear that we are dealing with sound.

[35]See A. Heidel, "Meaning of 'Mummu,'" 102; and J. Bottéro, *Mythes et rites*, 114, 117[4].

[36]The origin and etymology of Mummu have been much disputed, but the simplest solution is to consider it onomatopoeic. It denotes (1) "bleating", "noise" (*rigmu*), and (2) the ram-god (that makes exactly this noise). *Mummu* with the meaning "noise" is attested already in Ebla, where it glosses Sumerian g ù - ḫ ú l "cry of joy", cf. P. Fronzaroli, *Studi Eblaiti* III/3-4 (1980) 41 and M. Civil, ed., *Materials for the Sumerian Lexicon* XIII, Roma (1971), p. 246 7:6.

# BIBLIOGRAPHY TO THE PERSONAL STATEMENT

Allotte de la Fuÿe, Maurice, *Documents présargoniques* I (Paris, 1908). (Seal impressions of Lugalanda and his court.)

Andrae, Walter, *Das wiedererstandene Assur*, 2nd. ed. edited by Barthel Hrouda (München, 1977).

Barnett, Richard D., *Sculptures from the North Palace of Ashurbanipal at Nineveh (668–627 B.C.)* (London, 1976).

Behm-Blancke, M. R., *Das Tierbild in der altmesopotamischen Rundplastik*, Baghdader Forschungen I (Mainz, 1979), p. 53, for the present view concerning the origin of the "Sammelfund."

Caubet, Annie, "Un autel dédié par Nin Alla, épouse de Gudéa, don du Baron E. de Rothschild," *La Revue du Louvre et des Musées de France*, no. 1 (1991), pp. 14–17.

Christian, Viktor, *Altertumskunde des Zweistromlandes*

*von der Vorzeit bis zum Ende der Achäemeniden-herrschaft* (Leipzig, 1940).

Curtius, Ludwig, *Die Antike Kunst I, Ägypten und Vorderasien*, Handbuch der Kunstwissenschaft (Berlin, 1923).

Elmer-Dewitt, P., "The Golden Treasures of Nimrud," *Time* 134 (Oct. 30, 1989), pp. 80-81.

Falkenstein, Adam, *Archaische Texte aus Uruk*, (Berlin, 1936), Zeichenliste (283).

Frankfort, Henri, *The Art and Architecture of the Ancient Orient*, 4th rev. impression with additional bibliography (Baltimore, 1969), p. 47.

Frankfort, Henri, *Cylinder Seals: A Documentary Essay on the Art and Religion of the Ancient Near East* (London, 1939), p. 308.

Frankfort, Henri, *More Sculpture from the Diyala Region*, Oriental Institute Publications 60 (Chicago, 1943).

Heimpel, Wolfgang, "The Sun at Night and the Doors of Heaven in Babylonian Texts," *Journal of Cuneiform Studies* 38/2 (1986), pp. 127−151. The context of the phrase "lap of heaven" implies that the locality was found beneath the horizons.

Heinrich, Ernst, *Kleinfunde aus den archaischen Tempelschichten in Uruk*, Ausgrabungen der Deutschen Forschungsgemeinschaft in Uruk-Warka, Bd. 1 (Berlin, 1936).

Heuzey, Léon Alexandre, *Les origines orientales de l'art* (Paris, 1891−1915).

Koldewey, Robert, *Das wieder erstehende Babylon* (Leipzig, 1925).

Lenzen, Heinrich, XIV. *vorläufiger Bericht über die . . . Ausgrabungen in Uruk-Warka* (Berlin, 1958), pl. 42a.

Lenzen, Heinrich, "Ein Marmorkopf der Dschemdet Nasr-

# BIBLIOGRAPHY

Zeit aus Uruk," *Zeitschrift für Assyriologie und vorderasiatische Archäologie* 45 (1939), p. 85.

Matthews, Donald M., *Principles of Composition in Near Eastern Glyptic of the Later Second Millennium* B.C., *Orbis biblicus et orientalis.* Series Archaeologica 8 (Freiburg and Göttingen, 1990).

Menant, Joachim, *Les pierres gravées de la Haute-Asie* (Paris, 1883-1886).

Moortgat, Anton, *The Art of Ancient Mesopotamia* (London and New York, 1969), p. 62.

Pallis, S. A., *The Antiquity of Iraq* (Copenhagen, 1956), Chapter VI, list of excavations from 1842 onward.

Parrot, André, *Tello, vingt campagnes de fouilles (1877–1933)* (Paris, 1948).

Peters, J. P., *Nippur, or, Explorations and Adventures on the Euphrates,* 2 vols. (New York and London, 1897-98).

Porada, Edith, "Reliefs from the Palace of Sennacherib," *Bulletin of the Metropolitan Museum of Art,* Feb. 1945, pp. 152–160.

Porada, Edith, "Problems of Late Assyrian Reliefs," in *Essays in Ancient Civilization Presented to Helene J. Kantor,* A. Leonard and B. B. Williams, eds., Studies in Ancient Oriental Civilization 47 (Chicago, 1989), pp. 233–248.

Porada, Edith, "On the Problem of Kassite Art," in *Archaeologica Orientalia in Memoriam Ernst Herzfeld,* George C. Miles, ed. (Locust Valley, N.Y.), 1952, pp. 179–187.

Russell, John M., "Bulls for the Palace and Order in the Empire: The Sculptural Program of Sennacherib's Court VI at Nineveh," *The Art Bulletin* LXIX (1987), pp. 520–539.

Sarzec, Ernest de, *Découvertes en Chaldée* (Paris, 1884–1912).

Schäfer, Heinrich and Andrae, Walter, *Die Kunst des alten Orients*, Propyläen Kunstgeschichte II (Berlin, 1925).

Schlossman, Betty L., "Two Foundation Figurines," in *Ancient Mesopotamian Art and Selected Texts: The Pierpont Morgan Library* (New York, 1976), pp. 9–20. (Source of the photograph of the Ur-Nammu foundation figure.)

Severy, Merle, "Iraq, Crucible of Civilization," *National Geographic*, vol. 179, no. 5 (May 1991), pp. 102-111.

Strommenger, Eva, "Kunststeinfragment aus dem Riemchengebäude in Warka," *Baghdader Mitteilungen* 6, 1973), pp. 19–27.

Von der Way, Thomas, "Tell el Fara," in *Buto 2. Bericht.* Mitteilungen des Deutschen Archäologischen Instituts, Abt. Kairo 43 (1987), pp. 242–257.

Walker, C. B. F. and Hunger, H., "Zwölfmaldrei," *Mitteilungen der Deutschen Orient-Gesellschaft zu Berlin* 109 (1977), pp. 30–31, line 17.

Wiggermann, F. A. M., *Babylonian Prophylactic Figures: The Ritual Texts* (Amsterdam, 1986), *ugallu*, p. 331, *urmahlullû*, p. 332.

Wiggermann, F. A. M., "The Staff of Ninsubura: Studies in Babylonian Demonology," *Jaarbericht van het Vooraziatisch-Egyptisch Genootschaap Ex Oriente Lux*, no. 29 (1987), p. 24.

Winter, Irene J., "The Program of the Throneroom of Assurnasirpal II," in *Essays on Near Eastern Art and Archaeology in Honor of Charles Kyrle Wilkinson*, Prudence O. Harper and Holly Pittman, eds., (New York, 1983), pp. 15–31, fig. 6.

# BIOGRAPHICAL NOTES

EDITH PORADA was an art historian, archaeologist, educator, author, and editor. She was born in 1912 and grew up in Vienna where she wrote her thesis on Akkadian seals (ca. 2230–2190 B.C.) and obtained her doctorate in 1935. She moved to New York in 1938 and during the next ten years was awarded several prestigious research fellowships to continue her study of ancient Near Eastern cylinder seals and seal impressions. These fellowships included awards from The American Philosophical Society (1940–42, 1946), the American Schools of Oriental Research (1944), and the Bollingen Foundation (1947–49). During this time she catalogued the ancient seal impressions from the site of Nuzi, in Iraq (1947), and wrote two books on the seals in The Pierpont Morgan Library: her classic *Mesopotamian Art in Cylinder Seals* (1947), and her monumental *Corpus of Ancient Near Eastern Seals in North American Collections*, vol. I

(1948). In her *Corpus*, Edith Porada created a framework for scholars to determine date, style, and origin of cylinder seals, and is today still the standard reference work on seals.

Dr. Porada taught general art history at Queens College from 1950–1958. She came to Columbia University in 1958, and was made full professor in 1964. She was named Arthur Lehman Professor ten years later. In 1981, she was designated Lehman Professor Emeritus. In 1983, Columbia established a Chair in her honor: the Edith Porada Professorship of Ancient Near Eastern Art History and Archaeology. In 1989, Columbia awarded her the Honorary Degree of Doctor of Letters citing her "profound connections between the human experience and the interpretation of cylinder seals. For three decades you have inspired Columbia students with the beauty and wisdom of the Orient, leavened by your sparkling wit."

Edith Porada was awarded many honorary fellowships, memberships, and degrees, both in the United States and Europe. These honors were awarded by such renowned institutions as Smith College (Honorary Litt. D., 1967), American Academy of Arts and Letters (Fellow, 1969), the British Academy (Corresponding Fellow, 1977), American Philosophical Society (Member, 1978), the Austrian Academy of Sciences (Corresponding Member, 1980), and The Pierpont and Morgan Library (Honorary Fellow, 1980). Her many fellowships include two awards from the Guggenheim Foundation (1950, 1982–83). She received a gold medal for Distinguished Archaeological Achievement from the Archaeological Institute of America in 1977, and the Golden Horses of St. Mark Award from the Center for Studies and Research on Oriental Civilizations in Venice in 1988.

In the words of the Archaeological Institute's citation, Dr. Porada "has become the world's authority on ancient seals . . . She has opened the eyes and minds of archaeologists to the wealth of information on art, architecture, material culture, religious beliefs, mythology, economic, political, and intellectual life, cultural contacts, chronology, and history which are to be found on the seal stones with their miniature world of signs, images, intrinsic beauty, and testimony."

Since 1956, Edith Porada has been Honorary Curator of Seals and Tablets at The Pierpont Morgan Library. In addition to the great collection of cylinder seals of J. Pierpont Morgan housed at the Library, Dr. Porada built up a reference and study collection of modern impressions made by her of ancient seals in both public and private collections from around the world. During her tenure at the Library, she made these collections available to both scholars and the public: the Morgan Library became the primary center for cylinder seal research in the United States. Her seminars, given for Columbia University at the Morgan Library, have produced a number of well-trained, enthusiastic students, who now hold positions in universities and museums throughout the world. These students' publications bear witness to Dr. Porada's judicious advice and to her continued concern for creative Near Eastern scholarship.

In 1966, Dr. Porada founded the Columbia University Seminar for the Archaeology of the Eastern Mediterranean, Eastern Europe, and the Near East. She remained its chairwoman until her death. Her activities with Columbia, the Morgan Library, and the University Seminar regularly brought scholars in disparate fields together to investigate Near Eastern issues. One of her greatest legacies is the closely knit Near Eastern scholarly community in the New York area that was fostered by this continuous intercommunication.

Edith Porada published extensively. In addition to ten books, her publications include more than 100 articles and numerous book reviews. Her book, *The Art of Ancient Iran* (1965), covering a wide range of art history and archaeology from pre-history to the appearance of Islam remains the standard introduction to the field.

One of her final articles, "Why Cylinder Seals?" in the December 1993 *Art Bulletin*, brings the dating of styles and some of the bibliography for seal research up to the present, and at the same time aims at fostering appreciation for Near Eastern art among a nonspecialist audience.

Edith Porada studied archaeology because she wanted to learn about the origins of the human world of thought as they were revealed in images, engraved, sculptured or painted. Of equal interest to her was the course of thinking by archaeologists and historians of ancient art in the nineteenth and twentieth centuries. The influence of the general intellectual climate on modern scholars of the ancient Near East, and the history of that influence to the present day, was one of Edith Porada's great interests.

FRANCISCUS ANTONIUS MARIA WIGGERMANN was born in Amsterdam on the 10th of February 1948. The Jesuits taught him Greek and Latin at their Gymnasium (Ignatius College) in the same town, and from 1967 to 1974 he studied Semitic Language and Logic at the Free University of Amsterdam and at the Universities of Utrecht and Leyden. Since 1974 he teaches Assyriology at the Free University in Amsterdam. Meanwhile he was a collaborator of the *Chicago Assyrian Dictionary* at the Oriental Institute of the University of Chicago, and was a Fellow at the Metropolitan Museum of Art in New York. He wrote a book entitled *Mesopotamian Protective Spirits*, and a number of articles in various scholarly periodicals. He is married, and has two children.

RUTH NANDA ANSHEN is the author of *The Anatomy of Evil, Biography of an Idea, Morals Equals Manners* and *The Mystery of Consciousness: A Perscription for Human Survival.* She is a Fellow of the Royal Society of Arts of London, a member of the American Philosophical Association, the History of Science Society, the International Philosophical Society, and the Metaphysical Society of America.

The following was written by Professor Ernst Jäckh, Associate of Adenaner and Huess, Liberal Leaders of German Universal Culture in 1968:

> Dr. Ruth Nanda Anshen is a world-renowned philosopher. In 1958, she established the Anshen-Columbia University Seminars on the Nature of Man where some of the most emminent scholars gathered including: Albert Einstein (*in absentia*), Werner Heisenberg, Robert Oppenheimer, Jacque Maritain, Hanah Arendt, I.I. Rabi, Paul Tillich, Alexanderowich

Koyre, Pope John 23$^{rd}$, Samuel Terrein, Cardinal Bea, Radhakrishnan, Ambassador from India, Noam Chomsky, Lord Hugh Thomas of Swinerton, Sir Fred Hoyle, Sir Bernard Lovell, Edith Porada, Sir Muhamad Tafrulch Kahn, President of the World Court, Alfred North Whitehead, Jaroslav Pelikan, Roger Sperry, the great poet, Paul Goodman, Wittgenstein, Hermann Weyl, Hu Shih, Ambassador from China, Joseph Needham, Serge Alexander Koussevitsky, Andre Sakarov, Alexander Sacks, Harold Rosenberg, Bertrand Russell, Benedetto Croce, James Conant, Richard Courant, Niels Bohr, W.H. Auden, Donald Griffen, Morton Smith, Adolf Lowe, Karl Barth, Jean Pieget, J.B.S. Haldane, Jacques Hadamarh, Sir Julian Huxley, Erick Fromm, Taha Hussain, Robert Hutchins, and Gershom Scholem.

Dr. Anshen has the unique gift for gathering these leading scholars into a unity of purpose befitting their roles as the custodians of scholarship, knowledge, integrity, justice. First principles of morality as a heritage to the human mind and spirit were the common theme.

Dr. Anshen is the only living philosopher of the profound Olympian Greek and Roman tradition. As a bequest, she leaves for the human mind, spirit and soul what it means to be human.

Dr. Anshen's most recent achievement is the Anshen Transdisciplinary Lectureships in Art, Science and the Philosophy of Culture at the Frick Collection. Dr. Anshen's distinction as a scholar, philosopher and custodian herself of the Good, the True and the Beautiful by which mankind lives and has its being constitutes an immortal image of the human spirit, and should be so revered.

She has lectured in the leading universities of the Middle East, Japan, and Europe as well as in this country on the unitary principle of all reality.

# THE UNITY OF ART
# AND PHILOSOPHY

## RUTH NANDA ANSHEN

Before trying to answer to what extent we may speak of unity of knowledge, we may ask for the meaning of knowledge itself. It is not my intention to enter directly on an academic philosophical discourse for which I would hardly possess the required scholarship. Every philosopher however, is constantly confronted with the problem of objective description of experience with which, by definition, we shall understand communication in unambiguous terms. Our basic tool is plain language serving the needs of practical life and social intercourse. Here we shall not be concerned with studies of the origin of such language, but with its scope in scientific as well as philosophic communications. We will deal especially with the problem of how objectivity of description may be retained during the growth of experience beyond daily life events.

The main point is to realize that all knowledge is

originally represented within a conceptual framework adapted to account for previous experiences. Any such frame may prove too narrow to comprehend new experiences. Scientific research in many domains of knowledge has proved the necessity of abandoning or remoulding viewpoints which, due to their fruitfulness and apparently unrestricted applicability, were regarded as indispensable for rational explanation. Although such developments have been initiated by special studies, they entail a general lesson of importance just for the problem of unity of knowledge. The widening of the conceptual framework has served to restore order within the respective branches of knowledge. It also disclosed analogies in our position in regards to analysis and synthesis of experience in apparently separated domains of knowledge suggesting the possibility of an ever more embracing objective description.

When speaking of a conceptual framework we refer merely to unambiguous logical representation of relations between experiences. This attitude is also apparent in the historical development in which formal logic is no longer sharply distinguished from studies of semantics or even philological syntax. A special role, of course, is played by mathematics which has contributed so decisively to the development of logical thinking, and by its well-defined abstractions offers invaluable help in expressing harmonious relationships. Still, in our discussion, we shall not consider pure mathematics as a separate branch of knowledge. We will consider it as a refinement of general language supplementing it with appropriate tools of representing relations for whose communication ordinary verbal expression is either not sufficiently sharp or becomes too cumbersome. For the development of the so-called exact sciences characterized by the possibility of establishing numerical relationships, it has been of decisive importance to take recourse to abstract mathematical methods often developed without reference to such applications but originating from detached pursuit of generalizing logical constructions.

This situation is especially illustrated in philosophy, which was originally understood as all knowledge concerning that nature of which we ourselves are part, but gradually came to mean the study of the elementary laws governing the properties of animate matter. The necessity to pay constant attention to the problem of objective description has through the ages deeply influenced the attitude of philosophical schools. In our days, the exploration of new fields of experience has disclosed unsuspected presuppositions for the unambiguous application of some of our most elementary concepts, giving us an epistemological lesson with bearings on problems far beyond the domain of physical science. For our discussions it may therefore be convenient to start with a brief account of this development.

It would carry us too far to recall in detail how, after striving for the elimination of mythical cosmological ideas and arguments referring to the purposes of our own actions, the mechanical conception of nature developed in science with the pioneering work of Galileo and received such completion through Newton's elucidation of the principles and his mathematical mastership. Above all, the development of a deterministic description based on the possibility from the state of a physical system at a given instant, defined by measurable quantities, to predict its state at any subsequent time, meant a widegoing clarification of the problem of cause and effect. A so-called casual description of this kind came to stand as an ideal of scientific explanation in all domains of knowledge, irrespective of the way experience is obtained. Just in this connection, it is therefore important that the study of wider fields of physical experience has revealed the necessity of a closer consideration of the observational problem.

Within its immense field of application, classical mechanics presents an objective description in that sense that it is based on a well-defined use of pictures and ideas referring to daily life events. However rational the idealizations used in Newtonian mechanics might appear, they actually went far beyond the range of experience to which our elementary concepts are adapted. Thus, the adequate use of the very notions of absolute space and time is inherently connected with the practically instantaneous propagation of light, which allows us to locate the bodies around us independent of their velocities and to arrange events in a unique time sequence. The attempt at developing a consistent account of electromagnetic and optical phenomena revealed, however, that observers moving relatively to each other at high velocities will coordinate events differently. Such observers may not only take a different view of shapes and positions of rigid bodies, but also of events at separate points of space, which to one observer may appear as simultaneous but to another may be judged as occurring at different times.

The exploration of the extent to which the account of physical phenomena depends on the standpoint of the observer proved an invaluable guide in tracing general physical laws common to all observers. Retaining the idea of determinism, but relying only on relations between unambiguous measurements referring ultimately to coincidences of events, Einstein as far as I understand succeeded in remoulding and generalizing the whole edifice of classical physics, and in lending to our world picture a *unity* surpassing all previous expectations. In the general theory of relativity, the description is based on a curved four-dimensional space-time metric which automatically accounts for gravitational effects and the singular role of the speed of light signals representing an upper limit for any consistent use of the physical concept of velocity. The use of such unfamiliar but well defined mathematical abstractions does, indeed, in no way imply any departure from objective description, but offers rather an instructive illustration of how a widening of the conceptual framework affords the appropriate means of enlarging the scope of such description.

New unsuspected aspects of the observational problem should, however, be disclosed by the exploration of the atomic constitution of matter. The ideas of limited divisibility of substances, aiming at explaining the persistence of their characteristic properties in spite of the variety of natural phenomena, go back to antiquity. Close up to our days, such reviews were regarded as essentially hypothically in the sense that they seemed inaccessible to direct confirmation by observation on account of the coarseness of our sense organs and tools which themselves are composed of innumerable atoms. Still, with the great progress in chemistry and physics in the last centuries, atomic ideas proved ever more fruitful, and it was possible to obtain a general understanding of the principles of thermodynamics resting on a direct application of classical mechanics to the interaction of atoms and molecules during their incessant motions.

In this century, the study of newly discovered properties of matter, like natural radioactivity, had convincingly confirmed the fundamentals of atomic theory. Through the development of amplification devices it has been possible to study phenomena essentially dependent on single atoms, and even to obtain extensive knowledge of the structure of atomic systems. The first step was the recognition of the electron as a common constituent of all substances. An essential completion of our ideas of atomic constitution was obtained by Rutherford's discovery of the atomic nucleus containing within an extremely small volume almost the whole mass of the atom. The invariability of the elements in ordinary physical and chemical processes is directly interpreted by considering that, in such processes, although the electron binding may be largely influenced, the nucleus remains unaltered. By his demonstration of the transmutability of atomic nuclei by more powerful agencies, Rutherford, opened a quite new field of research, often referred to as modern alchemy, which, as is well-known, eventually should lead to the possibility of releasing immense amounts of energy stored in atomic nuclei.

Although many fundamental properties of matter were thus explained by the simple picture of the atom, from the beginning it was event that classical ideas of mechanics and electromagnetism did not suffice to account for the essential stability of atomic structures exhibited by the specific properties of the elements. A clue to the elucidation of this problem was afforded by the discovery of the universal quantum of action to which Planck was led in the first year of this century by his penetrating analysis of the laws of thermal radiation. This discovery revealed a feature of wholeness in atomic processes quite foreign to the mechanical conception of nature, and made it evident that the classical physical theories are idealizations valid only in the description of phenomena, in the analysis of which all actions are sufficiently large to permit the neglect of the quantum. While this condition is amply fulfilled in phenomena on the ordinary scale, we meet in atomic phenomena regularities of quite a new kind, defying deterministic pictorial description.

A rational generalization of classical physics, allowing for the existence of the quantum but retaining the unambiguous interpretation of experimental evidence defining inertial mass and electric charge of the electron and the nucleus, presented a very difficult task. By concerted efforts of a whole generation of theoretical physicists, a consistent and exhaustive description of atomic phenomena was, however, gradually developed. This description makes use of a mathematical formalism in which the variables in the classical physical theories are replaced by symbols subject to a non-commutable algorism involving Planck's constant. Due to the very character of such mathematical abstractions, the formalism does not allow pictorial representation on accustomed lines, but aims directly at establishing relations between observations obtained under well-defined conditions. Corresponding to the circumstance that several individual quantum processes may take place in a given experimental arrangement, these relations are of *inherently statistical character.*

By means of the quantum mechanical formalism, a detailed account of an immense amount of experimental evidence regarding the physical and chemical properties of matter has been achieved. Moreover, by adapting the formalism to the exigencies of relativistic invariance, it has been possible to order the rapidly growing new experience concerning the properties of elementary particles and the constitution of atomic nuclei. Notwithstanding the astounding power of quantum mechanics, the radical departure from accustomed physical explanation and especially the renunciation of the very idea of determinism have given rise to doubts in the minds of many physicists and philosophers whether we are dealing with a temporary procedure of expediency or whether we are confronted with an irrevocable step in regards to objective description. The clarification of this problem has actually demanded a radical revision of the foundation for the description and comprehension of physical experience.

In this connection, we must above all recognize how far the phenomena transcend the scope of classical physical theories, and that the account of the experimental arrangement and the recording of the observations must be given in plain language, suitably supplemented by technical physical terminology. This is a clear logical demand, since the very word "experiment" refers to a situation where we can tell others what we have done and what we have learned. The fundamental difference in regard to the analysis of the phenomena in classical and in quantum physics consists, however, in the circumstance that while in the former the interaction between the objects and the measuring instruments may be neglected or compensated for, the interaction between the atomic objects and the instruments which serve to define the experimental arrangement forms an integral part of quantum phenomena, as far as I understand. The impossibility of controlling this interaction is indeed an immediate consequence of the necessity of describing the functioning of these instruments on classical lines. Thus, although ultimately all physical experience is described by the concepts of classical physics, we cannot use such concepts as attributes of atomic objects independent of the way in which the phenomena are observed. The observer participates in the object observed.

In particular the impossibility in proper quantum phenomena of controlling the interaction between the objects and the measuring instruments prevents the unrestricted combination of space-time coordination and dynamic conservation laws on which the deterministic description in classical physics rests. In fact, any unambiguous use of the concepts of space and time refers to an experimental arrangement involving a transfer of momentum and energy, uncontrollable in principle, to the instruments like measuring rods and synchronized clocks, required for the fixation of the reference frame. Conversely, the account of phenomena governed by conservation of momentum and energy involves in principle a renunciation of detailed space-time coordination. These circumstances find quantitative expression in Heisenberg's indeterminacy relations which specify the reciprocal latitude for the fixation of kinematical and dynamical variables in the definition of the state of a physical system in the quantum mechanical formalism. In accordance with the very character of this formalism such relations cannot, however, be interpreted in terms of attributes of objects referring to classical pictures. But here we are dealing with the mutually exclusive conditions for the unambiguous use of the concepts of space and time, on the one hand, and dynamical conservation laws, on the other.

The essential wholeness of proper quantum phenomena finds logical expression in the circumstance that any attempt at a well-defined subdivision would require a change in the experimental arrangement prohibitive for the appearance of the phenomenon we set out to analyze. Moreover, it is essential for the definition of the phenomena that they are brought to a close, represented by a permanent mark on a photographic plate recording the impact of an electron or similar observations obtained by suitable amplification devices of essentially irreversible functioning. We have here to do with a fundamental feature of objective description which in classical science finds its counter-part in the presupposition that every stage in the course of the phenomenon is represented by a state of the system defined by measurable quantities. Further, the unlimited freedom of experimentation, presupposed in classical science, corresponds to the free choice of experimental arrangements and thereby of the atomic phenomena to be investigated.

The synthesis of experiences obtained under different experimental conditions presents us, however, with a fundamentally novel relationship. In fact, such phenomena, which from the point of view of deterministic pictorial description may appear as contradictory, are to be regarded as complementary, in the sense that they represent equally important aspects of, and together exhaust, the knowledge obtainable about the atomic objects. The notion of complementarity is merely to be regarded as the logical expression for our position as regards objective description in this field of experience. The crucial point is to realize the role which the measuring tools play for the unambiguous use of our most elementary concepts, and the limitation thereby set to the applicability of the very idea of causality adapted to the practical account of daily life events. Of course, we also retain our position as detached observers, but the section line defining the content of objective description must in each case be suitably drawn to permit the definition of the concepts by which experience is described.

As regards the much debated question of the demands to physical explanation it must be borne in mind that already the mechanical conception of nature implied the renunciation on cause of uniform motion and that especially relativity theory has taught us how arguments of invariance and equivalence must be counted as categories of rational explanation. Similarly, in quantum physics we have a further well defined generalization which embraces fundamental regularities implying a limited scope of the presuppositions of deterministic description. The circumstance that in general one and the same experimental arrangement may yield different recordings pertaining to a closed indivisible phenomenon is sometimes picturesquely described as a choice of nature between such possibilities. Of course, one is here not in any way alluding to a personification of nature, but rather pointing to the logical impossibility under such conditions to look for directives on accustomed casual lines.

The whole history of physical science has indeed taught us how the exploration of ever wider fields of experience reveals unsuspected limitations of accepted ideas and points to a freer attitude necessary to restore order and harmony. As we shall proceed to show, the epistemological lesson contained in the development of atomic physics allows us to trace similar situations as regards analysis and synthesis of experience far beyond the borders of physical science, and to ascertain common features promoting the search for unity of knowledge.

The first problem with which we are confronted is the question of the place of the living organisms in the description of natural phenomena. Originally, no sharp distinction between animate and inanimate matter was made, and it is well-known that Aristotle, in stressing the wholeness of the individual organisms, opposed the views of the atomists and even in the discussion of the foundations of mechanics retained ideas like purpose and potency. However, with the great discoveries in anatomy and physiology at the time of the Renaissance, and especially with the advent of classical mechanics, from the deterministic description of which any reference to purpose is eliminated, a completely mechanistic conception of nature suggested itself, and a large number of organic functions could in fact be accounted for by the same physical and chemical properties of matter which found widegoing explanation in atomic theory. It is true that the ordering of atomic processes involved in such mechanisms was sometimes difficult to reconcile with the laws of thermodynamics, implying a steady approach towards disorder among the atoms constituting an isolated physical system. If, however, sufficient account is taken of the circumstance that the free energy necessary to maintain and develop the organic systems is continually supplied from their surroundings by nutrition and respiration, it becomes clear that there is in such respect no question of any violation of general physical laws, as well as philosophical implications.

Still, in spite of the wide field of application of classical physical ideas in physiology, such ideas offer no direct approach to the evolution and maintenance of self-regulating entities like the living organisms. Our problem is rather to explore the possibilities for a widening of the conceptual frame required for an objective description of typical biological phenomena. In this connection, the general lesson derived from the study of atomic processes provides a new background for our inquiry. From the outset, it is evident that quantum regularities are decisive for the properties of the atoms and chemical molecules of which the organisms, just as inanimate bodies like our tools, are built. They in particular are required for the stability of the highly complex molecular structures, which form the essential constituents in the cells responsible for the hereditary properties of the species. Moreover, the researches about mutations which can be produced by exposure of the organisms to penetrating radiation offer a striking application of the *statistical laws* of atomic physics but not of philosophy. Also the sensitivity of perceptive organs, so important for the integrity of the organism, has been found to approach the level of individual quantum processes. Clearly amplification mechanisms, reminding of the recording devices used in experiments of atomic physics, play an important part especially in the transmission of nervous messages although unrelated to philosophy.

Notwithstanding the promising development in such respects, it is nevertheless obvious that the element of individuality represented by the quantum of action offers no direct analogy to the essential wholeness of a living organism. Indeed, the characteristic features of self-regulation and adaptation of the organisms to the environment cannot be exhaustively accounted for by the regularities governing the closed indivisible quantum processes whose very definition demands an experimental arrangement prohibitive for the appearance of phenomena displaying such features. Just this circumstance, however, demands a freer attitude to the description of proper biological phenomena. When, in this connection, we may allude to life as an experiment of nature itself, we are no more than in atomic physics, invoking mysticism but rather stressing our position as regards objective description. Actually, we must recognize that the requirements of such description, at least in tendency, are fulfilled by the characteristic complementary way in which arguments, based on the full resources of physical and chemical science, and concepts directly referring to the wholeness of the organism transcending the scope of these sciences, are practically used in biological research and possess philosophical qualities.

The appropriateness of the notion of complementarity for the comprehension of biological phenomena is not least apparent in the studies of such innate and conditioned *behaviour of animals and man,* to the description of which psychological concepts most readily lend themselves. Of course, in ethology, as in all proper physical and biological research, we keep to our detached position as observers, and are only referring to the indispensability of such terminology even in an allegedly pure behaviouristic approach. It would carry us too far to attempt any sharp distinction between the use of such words as instinct and reason, which point to situations mutually excluding each other as illustrated by the extent to which instinctive behaviour is suppressed by the demands of life in human societies. As regards the concept of the human mind, we may, as far as we can communicate our thoughts and sentiments by language, speak of an objective description of psychical experiences. It is interesting to note that, while in the early stages of physical science, one could directly rely on such features of daily life events which permitted simple casual account, an essentially complementary description of the content of our mind has been used since the origin of languages.

The rich terminology adapted to such communication does not point to an unbroken course of events, but rather to separate mutually exclusive experiences. An especially striking example is offered by the relationship between situations where we are pondering motives for our actions and where we experience a feeling of violition. We are obviously here concerned with a different placing of the section line between the content on which attention is focused and the background indicated by the very word "ourselves." In normal life, this situation is more or less intuitively recognized, but symptoms characterized as confusion of the "egos" which may lead to dissolution of personality are well-known in psychiatry. The use in psychology of apparently contrasting attributes referring to equally important aspects of the human personality presents a remarkable analogy to the situation in philosophy where complementary phenomena are defined by different elementary concepts.

Above all, a comparison between conscious experiences and physical observations suggests itself that the very word "conscious" refers to features of the mind capable of retainment in the memory like the premanency of recording in atomic phenomena. In such analogy, the obscurity inherent in the idea of subconsciousness corresponds to the impossibility of pictorial interpretation of the quantum mechanical formalism which, in principle, serves merely in ordering of well-defined observations. Incidentally, medical use of psycho-analytical treatment in curing neurosis may rather be said to restore balance in the content of the memory of the patient by bringing him new conscious experience, than helping him to fathom the abysses of his subconsciousness, as I learn.

From a biological point of view, we can hardly interpret the characteristics of psychical phenomena except by concluding that every well-defined conscious experience corresponds to a residual impression of the organism, involving an irreversible process of some similar kind as in the amplification devices used in the storing of information in electronic calculation machines. Such machines present a striking similarity with an organism which on information received through its receptive organs, after complicated processes in the brain influenced by earlier experiences, responds by nervous messages to its motoric organs. Quite apart from the circumstance that every step in the working of a calculating machine is in principle open to observation and control, while in the functioning of the organism we have to do with a feature of wholeness not analyzable in such terms, it would not be appropriate in connection with the machine to use the word "mind." Not only is the conception of consciousness not directly implied in the objective description of the machine, but in speaking of the state of our mind we are in practice especially referring to aspects of contemplative introspection, where we are not immediately concerned with physical phenomena involved in actions or communication.

As regards the difficulty of avoiding ambiguities in such discussion, it is important to realize the different starting points when approaching physical and psychical phenomena. While physical observations are ordered with direct reference to the experimental conditions, we have in psychical experience to do with separate observations whose correlation can only be indicated by their belonging to the wholeness of the mind. In return, all knowledge, including that of physical sciences, is of course ultimately comprised in our consciousness. In this connection we must above all recognize that the logical concepts needed for objective description are the simpler the more restricted is the field of experience concerned. While in physical phenomena explicit reference is only made to material objects and tools of observation, we have in the account of psychical experience to do with a further shifting of the object-subject section line, and as regards the elimination of contradictions it is suggestive that the simpler concepts of objective description of natural phenomena to an ever higher degree lose their applicability the more we approach those features of living organisms which are related to the working of our mind.

To illustrate such argumentation, we may refer to the old problem of free will. From what has already been said, it is evident that the word "volition" is indispensable in an exhaustive description of psychical phenomena, but the problem is how far we can speak of a freedom to act according to our possibilities. As long as one takes unrestricted deterministic views, or believes in universal predestination, any idea of such freedom is of course excluded. However, the general lesson of atomic physics, and in particular of the limited scope of mechanistic description of biological phenomena, suggest the idea that the potency of organisms to adjust themselves to the environment includes the power of selecting the most appropriate way to this purpose. In view of the impossibility of judging such matters on purely physical basis, it is most important to recognize that psychical experience may offer more pertinent information about the problem.

The decisive point is here that, if we attempt to predict what another person will decide to do in a given situation, we must of course not only strive to know his whole background, including the story of his life in all respects which may have contributed to form his character, but we must realize that what we are ultimately aiming at is to place ourselves in his position. Although it is impossible to say whether a person wants to do something because he believes he can, or whether he can because he will, it is hardly disputable that we have the feeling of so-to-say being able to make the best out of the circumstances. From the point of view of objective description, nothing can here be added or taken away, and in this sense we may both practically and logically speak of the freedom of our will in a way which leaves the proper latitude for the use of words like "responsibility" and "hope", which themselves are just as much and as little definable as are other words indispensable in human communications.

In any attempt at further elucidation of our position we cannot avoid the paradoxes inherent in an expression like explanation of ourselves and strikingly illustrated in the divergent attitudes of different philosophical schools. I need only briefly remind you of the dualistic view of Descartes, according to which the organisms are compared with machines, taken literally in the case of animals, while our own body is regarded more as a mechanical tool used for the information of the human soul about the material world and as its agency of reacting on such information. It is also well-known how Spinoza attempted a monastic view eliminating all interaction between body and soul by pointing to a parallelism between the functioning of our bodies and the working of the mind regarded as two attributes of one and the same substance. Of course, in our days, it is evident that the special assumptions of Descartes on the location of the inter-action between body and soul are irreconcilable with anatomical and physiological studies of the nervous system, and that Spinoza's approach to biological and psychological problems does not conform with subse-quent explorations of the conditions for objective de-scription in these fields of experience. However, we appreciate Descartes' famous words "cogito ergo sum" as a recognition of the indispensability of the idea of mind, and likewise we are in Spinoza's attitude reminded of essential difficulties regarding our observational posi-tion. In attempting an all-embracing account of our situ-ation we approach the very limit of objective description which demands a well defined section line between object and observer and therefore in principle exclude the notion of an ultimate subject. The ambiguities of language with which we are here confronted are illustrated in the academic discussions of questions like the existence of the world around us and of consciousness of other persons, the answers to which are of course presupposed as regards the needs of practical communication.

So far I have endeavoured to present, or at any rate to touch upon, some of the main problems in science and of course philosophy to be discussed at this conference on the unity of knowledge. On our program, however, the question is raised whether, distinct from scientific truth, there is a poetic or spiritual or cultural truth, and with all recluctance of a philosopher to enter into such fields, I shall venture from a similar attitude as that indicated in the preceding to make some comments also on this question. Taking up the argument of the relation between our means of expression and the extension of the field of experience with which we are concerned, we are indeed directly confronted with the relationship of science and art. The enrichment which art can give us originates just in its power of reminding us of harmonies beyond the grasp of systematic analysis. Literary, pictorial and musical art form a sequence of modes of expression, where the ever more widegoing renunciation on definition characteristic of scientific communication permits us to leave the phantasy a freer play.

In their means of expression the artists can, however, only rely on inspiration based on common human experience, and even at the climax of their work we recognize the common foundation on which we stand. In particular, we must realize that a word like "improvisation", so readily on our tongue when speaking of artistic achievements, points to a feature essential in all communication. Not only are we in ordinary conversation more or less unaware of the verbal expressions we are going to choose in communicating what is on our mind, but even in written papers where we have the possibility to reconsider every word, the question whether we shall leave it stand or change it, demands for its answer a final decision essentially equivalent with an improvisation. Moreover, in the balance between seriousness and humour, characteristic of all truly artistic achievements, we witness complementary aspects, conspicuous in children's plays and no less appreciated in mature life. Indeed, if we endeavoured always to speak quite seriously, we run the risk very soon to our listeners and ourselves to appear ridiculously tedious, but if we try to joke all the time, we rapidly bring ourselves and our listeners too—if the witticisms have some points—in the desperate mood which Shakespeare with such genius has pictured for us in the role of the jesters in his immortal dramas.

In a comparison between science and art, we must of course realize that, in the former, we have to do with systematic concerted efforts of augmenting experience and developing appropriate concepts resembling the carrying of stones to a building while, in the latter, we are presented with more intuitive individual efforts of evoking sentiments recalling the wholeness of our situation.